GRAND SUMO
FULLY ILLUSTRATED

Edited by PHP INSTITUTE, INC.
Supervising Editor: Seigoro Kitade
Translator: Deborah Iwabuchi

D0901506

YOHAN PUBLICATIONS, INC.

GRAND SUMO
FULLY ILLUSTRATED

Published April 1998

Copyright ©1998 Seigoro Kitade & PHP Institute, Inc.

Planning and Production: Toru Ishida
Main Illustrations: Koji Sakurada, Mayumi Yamamura and Izumi Oda
Other Illustrations: Teruyoshi Kojima and Mayumi Sasaki
Cover Design: Art Construction Center (ACC)

YOHAN PUBLICATIONS, INC.
14-9 Okubo 3-chome, Shinjuku-ku, Tokyo, Japan

Printed in Japan

Author's Preface

In the past, sumo was primarily the domain of the older set. Nowadays, however, it has become popular with young people as well. Because the upcoming rikishi all have formidable strength and the bouts are fierce, sumo promises to continue to be popular for many years to come.

Sumo has a long tradition of complicated customs and difficult vocabulary. This book contains the basics on these in an illustrated format that can be read as a book and/or used as a referenceguide.

Because I've always felt that this knowledge of sumo should not be the exclusive property of a small number of fans, I've written this book so that as many people as possible can learn about, understand and enjoy the wonderful sport of sumo.

Seigoro Kitade
August 1993

Translator's Preface

The first thing a potential fan browsing through shelves of books on sumo may want to know is how useful this one is. The answer is "very useful," and the proof is that, while translating this book (and Yohan's first sumo publication, *Sumo Watching*) my family spent a lot of time watching sumo on TV and we also attended grand sumo touring events that came to our town. Whenever anyone had a question about sumo, including my mother-in-law, a life-long sumo fan, I was the one who always had the answer. And the reason I knew was usually because I had read it in this book. Anyone who is interested in sumo and the least bit nosy will find a treasure trove of information here on the public and private lives of sumo wrestlers: how careers are launched, who gets paid how much, where they buy their underwear, whether they do their own hair, and much, much more. Learn about the supporting roles of gyoji and all sorts of behind-the-scenes information. There is so much more to sumo than what we see on TV or live at the tournament halls. Explanations in the book are all accompanied by illustrations that make the book interesting and enjoyable to read.

Although the world of sumo has plenty of secrets, it is open and available to the public to a surprising degree. I enjoy listening to the English-language broadcasts of the sumo tournaments on the NHK satellite channel. The announcers often talk about chatting with rikishi, watching practice sessions, and so on. So, with my new-found expertise in hand, I decided to take a trip to the Ryogoku area in Tokyo.

When you leave the Ryogoku Station, the first thing you see is the enormous Kokugikan. Although the main hall was not open, I was able to visit the Sumo Museum, a small display of photographs and *kesho-mawashi* of yokozuna of yesteryear. After lunch at one of the numerous *chanko nabe* restaurants, I received a map of the area from the waiter and visited the shops mentioned in this book. There is Lion-do that sells rikishi-size clothes, and Kikuya the *tabi* maker, which has a window-front museum of the Japanese-style socks they have made for the various rikishi, past and present. The tiny Sumo Photography Museum was closed the day I visited, but the owner was happy to unlock the door, show me his work and talk about his own experiences taking pictures of rikishi, dating back to the father and uncle of yokozuna Takanohana. He also gave me a *banzuke* ranking chart before sending me on my way. The friendly proprietor of Okada-ya, the shop that supplies rikishi with *geta*, showed me the size (33.5 centimeters) and style of formal sandal that Akebono often orders. He told me that a yokozuna frequently attends functions that require formal kimono and *hakama* attire, and that he must always have an impeccable appearance. Formal *geta* can only be worn a few times before they have to be replaced with a new, clean pair. Extending this idea to the *tabi* shop it suddenly became clear to me why such a limited clientele could keep these enterprises in business. Even though I did not meet or even catch sight of any of my favorite rikishi, I felt as though I had had a small but satisfying taste of the lives they lead.

Read this book, and you may discover, as I did, that a little bit of knowledge on sumo may be your key to enjoyment of many more aspects of the sport. I hope that you have as much fun reading it as I did working on the translation.

I would like to give special thanks to my good friend Kazuko Enda for her time and expertise in dealing with some of the more difficult terms, especially the seventy winning moves.

Deborah Iwabuchi
January 1998
Maebashi, Japan

Contents

The Supporters of Sumo   113

Unryu Type

What is Sumo?

The History of Sumo I
From the Age of Myths
Through the Edo Era

Akeni

[Age of Myths]

- The gods Takemikazuchi and Takeminakata fight each other at Inasahama in the Izumo District (present-day Shimane Prefecture). *1
- Nominosukune battles Taimanokehaya in Yamato (present-day Nara Prefecture). This is considered to be the first sumo bout. *2

Myths and legends concerning sumo are included in the two best-known histories of ancient Japan, the Kojiki and Nihon Shoki. From these legends it is believed that sumo was used to predict and pray for bountiful harvests, as well as to interpret the will of the spirits of the dead.

[Nara and Heian Eras]

642	Soldiers are invited to wrestle for the privilege of serving Kudara, an ancient Korean governor. This is the earliest historical record of sumo. *2
726	Exhibition sumo matches are held at shrines of Emperor Shomu. (Earliest record of sumo for religious purposes.)
734	Emperor Shomu views sumo. (Earliest record of an emperor observing sumo.) *3
793	Emperor Kanmu views sumo. At about this time, the custom of annual sumo matches at the imperial palace begins.
810	Emperor Saga views sumo.
821	The ceremonial rituals of *sumo sechie* (held each year in July), where the emperor would watch sumo at his palace and then hold a party for his servants, are prescribed in the Dairishiki, the book of rules for various imperial ceremonies and events.
869	Sumai-no-sechi is formally established as an official seasonal celebration in the Jogan Kyakushiki.
1174	Emperor Takakura views sumo. *Sumo sechie* is held for the first time in fifteen years. After this, however, the Genji and Heike clans gain power and the custom is abolished. Sumo enters the age of the samurai.

Sumo sechie was begun as an imperial ceremony in the year 734 when the matches were first witnessed by the Emperor Shomu. This regular event continued for 400 years, through the reign of Emperor Takakura in 1174.

[Age of the Samurai]

1189	Shogun Minamoto-no-Yoritomo views sumo at Tsurugaoka Hachimangu in Kamakura. Sumo viewing by the shogun becomes a frequent event. *4
1257	Shogun Hojo Tokiyori views sumo. *4 After this, sumo declines in popularity for about three hundred years. This, then, becomes the age of provincial sumo training.

Sources: *1 *Kojiki*   *2 *Nihon Shoki*   *3 *Shoku Nihongi*   *4 *Azuma Kagami* (a history of samurai society edited by the Kamakura government.)

The purpose of sumo has changed through the ages. During the Nara and Heian eras it was event held in the imperial palace. From the Kamakura Era (1192-1333) through the Era of Warring States (1473-1573), it was a form of training for samurai. During the Edo Era, sumo was a popular form of entertainment used to raise money for temples and shrines. Presented below is a brief history of sumo from mythological times through the Edo Era (1603-1867).

1570	Oda Nobunaga holds exhibition sumo at Jorakuji Temple. *5 It then becomes a frequent event.
1596	A group of ten sumo wrestlers from the Kansai region travels to Kyushu to hold matches. *6 The first professional sumo wrestlers emerge toward the end of the Ashikaga Era.
1605	Sumo matches are held to benefit shrines and temples at Yamashiro Daigo in Kyoto. *7

Sumo was practiced widely as a form of training for samurai. Matches were often held for the shogun and were also popular among the general citizenry. During the Era of Warring States, sumo was performed for the pleasure of provincial daimyo. it was at the close of this era that the first professional sumo wrestlers emerged.

[Edo Era]

1645	Authorized benefit sumo *(kanjin-sumo)* is held at Kyoto's Tadasu-no-Mori. *8
1648	Amateur and benefit sumo are officially banned because of fights over the bouts that break out between gangsters and unemployed samurai.
1684	Benefit sumo is held at Edo's Fukagawa Hachiman Temple. Benefit sumo is once again officially authorized. Amateur sumo, however, is frequently banned.
1699	A wooden ranking chart is displayed for benefit sumo held at Kyoto's Okazaki Tenno-sha Shrine. *9 This is the earliest record of a *banzuke* ranking chart. It is also the first time the names of the three highest sumo ranks appear.
1757	The distinct vertical sumo ranking chart of the Edo Era is issued for the first time. From this time, the *kanza* system of Edo sumo begins to take hold.
1789	Tanikaze Kajinosuke and Onogawa Kisaburo receive yokozuna licenses from the Yoshida Tsukasa family. (This is the first official yokozuna.)
1791	The eleventh shogun, Tokugawa Ienari, views sumo at Edo Castle.
1833	From the October tournament until the Ryogoku Kokugikan Hall is completed in 1901, the Honjo Ekoin Temple is the official location for sumo tournaments.
1854	Sumo wrestlers demonstrate to the Americans their enormous strength by carrying bales of rice onto Admiral Perry's Black Ships anchored at Yokohama.

Sumo as we know it was gradually established during this period. An organization, the Sumo Kaisho, was formed to handle benefit sumo, and daimyo began to run their own sumo stables. At the end of this era the legendary wrestlers Tanikaze, Onogawa, and Raiden came onto the scene, and Edo benefit sumo emerged as a sport popular among all classes of people.

*5 *Nobunaga-ko-ki*   *6 *Gizangokaku*   *7 *Gienjungo-nikki*   *8 *Kokon-sumo-taizen*
*9 *Oe-shunko-ki*

The History of Sumo I
Meiji and Taisho Eras

Agemaki

[Meiji Era]

1868	April	The Meiji Emperor views Kyoto wrestlers at the Zama Shrine in Osaka.
1869	November	The Takasago Incident. Takasago Uragoro presses for reform of the sumo system and is subsequently expelled from the Sumo Kaisho association. Takasago creates an independent organization and heads for the Kansai region.
1878	February	The police department distributes regulations for wrestlers (rikishi) and referees (gyoji). Rikishi, gyoji, and elders receive business licenses.
	May	The reformed Takasago organization is revived and merges with the Sumo Kaisho in Tokyo, which begins issuing its own ranking chart.
1889	January	Reform of the sumo regulations. The Sumo Kaisho is renamed the Tokyo Grand Sumo Association. The number of stockholding elders is limited to 88.
1890	May	The word "yokozuna" appears on the ranking chart for the first time. The wrestler in this position is Nishinoumi Kajiro.
1896	January	The Nakamura Ro Incident. The west-side rikishi Odohira and thirty-two other wrestlers file a complaint with Sumo Kaisho and press for reform. The reforms are made and implemented the following month.
1909	February	Yokozuna and ozeki are officially declared the top two sumo ranks.
	June	The Ryogoku Kokugikan Hall is built. Tournaments are no longer scheduled for ten days of fair weather, because, for the first time, they can be held indoors for ten consecutive days, rain or shine. Makuuchi wrestlers, who had been allowed to sit out the final day of competition, now compete in all ten days of every tournament. The east-west competition system is revised and a championship flag introduced. Haori jackets are ruled mandatory for *sekitori* (a term that refers to all wrestlers juryo rank and above) entering the tournament hall.
1910	May	The costume of the gyoji is changed.
1911	January	Makuuchi rikishi barricade themselves in the Shimbashi Club over a salary dispute. The matter is settled shortly thereafter.

Rikishi, released by their daimyo masters after the Meiji Reformation, began organizing themselves into sumo associations, and the Tokyo Grand Sumo Association was founded in 1888. In 1909, the Ryogoku Kokugikan was built, and changes in the system followed thick and fast. The ten-day tournament was established, the east-west competition begun, and so on.

Haridashi Information	There were originally three different sets of kanji for the word "sumo." The present day kanji, 相撲, were not widely used until 1926.

After the Meiji Reformation, when the land and subjects of the samurai were returned to the emperor, homeless rikishi organized themselves into the Tokyo Sumo Association. The organization was revised many times in succeeding years as the foundation for the association as we know it was created. In the chart below is a chronological listing of significant events during the Meiji and Taisho eras.

[Taisho Era]

1914	June	The rikishi Tachiyama and Otori make a tour of Hawaii.
1915	August	The rikishi Umegatani and Nishinoumi make a tour of the U.S.A.
1917	November	The Kokugikan is destroyed by fire.
1920	January	Kokugikan is rebuilt and the opening ceremony held.
1921	June	The rikishi Onishiki and Tochigiyama make a tour of Hawaii and the U.S.A.
1923	January	The Mikawashima Disturbance. Before a tournament, the rikishi decide to demand an increase in pensions, and barricade themselves in the Mikawashima Electrolysis Plant. The association accepts the demand and increases the length of tournaments to eleven days to raise the amount necessary for the extra payments.
	September	Kokugikan is destroyed by fire in the wake of the Great Kanto Earthquake.
1925	April	Sumo for imperial viewing is held to celebrate the installation of Crown Prince Hirohito as emperor. The winner's cup is established with the money consequently received from the new emperor.
	December	Permission is received from the Ministry of Education to create a juridical foundation, and thus the Japan Grand Sumo Association Juridical Foundation is born.
1926	January	The last official tournament of the Osaka Grand Sumo Association is held in Taipei.
	July	The Tokyo and Osaka associations disband based on an agreement to sign the charter of the Japan Grand Sumo Association.

Reform and modernization of the sumo system continued, and the foundation for the present-day organization laid. In 1925, the Tokyo Grand Sumo Association received permission to establish the Japan Grand Sumo Association Juridical Foundation. This was also the occasion for the dissolution of the separate Tokyo and Osaka associations as they merged into a single body.

Showa and Heisei Era Grand Sumo I
1926 to 1952

[The Birth of the Japan Grand Sumo Association]

1927	January	The Tokyo and Osaka sumo associations merge into the Japan Grand Sumo Association. Four official tournaments are held each year. The number of stockholding elders includes 88 from Tokyo and 17 from Osaka, including two one-generation stockholders, for a total of 105.
1928	January	*Shikiri* (pre-bout face-off) time is limited to ten minutes for makuuchi ranks, seven minutes for juryo, and five minutes for makushita. The *shikiri* lines are also established. All juryo rikishi now compete on all eleven tournament days. Radio broadcasts of tournaments begin.
	March	The default system is established, applicable to all rikishi in makushita, juryo, and makuuchi ranks.
1931	April:	On the occasion of a viewing by the emperor, the size of the ring is increased, the double ring changed to a single one 4.55 meters in diameter, and the roof over the ring is refashioned into a Shinto style.
1932	January	The Shunjuen Incident. All of the rikishi of the West Dewanoumi stable, with sekiwake Tenryu as their leader, call for sumo reform, banding themselves into a group they call the Shinko Rikishi Dan (New Rikishi Organization). They barricade themselves into Shunjuen, a Chinese restaurant. In response, some east-side rikishi form a similar group and leave the sumo association. These actions cause the cancellation of the January tournament.
	February	The association rewrites the ranking chart using the names of the remaining rikishi. They abandon the east-west competition and hold an eight-day tournament with competition between stables and individual rikishi.
1933	January	As most of the rikishi return to the association, two ranking charts are prepared; one for the returnees and one for rikishi who never left, with separate competitions held.
	February	Rikishi who have not returned found the Kansai Sumo Association. The Japan Grand Sumo Association cancels its tournaments in the Kansai region and reverts to two official tournaments a year, one each in spring and fall.
1937	May	The thirteen-day tournament is established.
	December	The Kansai Sumo Association disbands.
1939	May	The fifteen-day tournament is established.
1940	January	East-west competition resumes.

In January 1927, the east and west sumo associations were merged into the Japan Grand Sumo Association. Various changes were instituted, including limitations on *shikiri* time, an enlargement of the ring, change from a double to a single ring, and so on. The rikishi Futabayama was promoted to yokozuna and the sport attained new heights of popularity.

Haridashi Information	In 1949, the number of tournaments was increased from two to three a year. It was increased to four in 1953, and five in 1957. The current schedule of six tournaments a year was begun in 1958.

In 1927, the east and west sumo associations were unified into one, and the predecessor of the current sumo association was born. The rules and regulations of the association were consequently reformed, gradually evolving into the present-day system. The chart below includes the major developments in sumo between the years 1926 (the first year of the Showa Era) and 1952.

[World War II]

1942	January	*Shikiri* time is shortened: seven minutes for makuuchi, five minutes for juryo, and three minutes for makuuchi.
1944	May	Because the Kokugikan is requisitioned by the Imperial Army in February, a ten-day tournament is held at the Korakuen baseball stadium.
1945	March	Kokugikan is destroyed in an air raid. Many sumo stables are also destroyed.
	November	The first post-war tournament is held in the ruins of the Kokugikan, held on ten fair-weather days. *Shikiri* time is shortened to five minutes for makuuchi, four minutes for juryo, and three minutes for makuuchi.
	December	The Kokugikan is requisitioned by the Occupation Army.
1948	October	The first post-war eleven-day tournament is held in the provisional Kokugikan in Osaka.
1950	May	The Yokozuna Judging Committee is established.
	September	*Shikiri* time is shortened to four minutes for makuuchi, three minutes for juryo, and two minutes for makuuchi.
1952	January	The rikishi banners that decorate the outside of the Kokugikan during tournaments are used for the first time since the end of the war. The bow-twirling ceremony is now held at the end of each tournament day.
	April	The Memorial Hall (Kokugikan) is returned by the Occupation Army.
	September	The four poles supporting the roof over the ring are removed and it is suspended from the ceiling.

War in the Pacific broke out in 1941. The Kokugikan was destroyed in the great air raids on Tokyo in March 1945. During this same period, most of the sumo stables were also destroyed and official activities were temporarily canceled. In November 1945, only a few months after the end of the war, tournaments were resumed, the first one taking place in the ruins of the Ryogoku Kokugikan.

Showa and Heisei Era Grand Sumo II
1953 to 1993

Eboshi

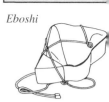

[The Curtain is Raised on Modern Sumo]

1953	January	Four official tournaments a year: January (First), March (Spring), May (Summer), and September (Fall), with the March tournament held in Osaka.
	May	First live television broadcast of a sumo tournament.
1954	September	Opening ceremony for the new Kuramae Kokugikan, and opening of the Sumo Museum.
1955	May	First visit to a sumo tournament at the new Kokugikan by the Showa Emperor. This is the first imperial viewing in eighteen years.
1956	January	The pre-sumo system that has been abandoned since the Fall 1946 Tournament is revived from the sixth day.
1957	January	With the addition of a tournament in Kyushu in November, the number of official tournaments is increased to five a year.
	May	Revision of salaries of rikishi and elders. Establishment of a monthly salary system.
	July	The decision is made to demote ozeki with losing records for three consecutive tournaments.
	October	Establishment of a sumo training school, with training periods to last six months.
1958	January	A Nagoya tournament is scheduled for July and the number of tournaments increases to six a year. The name of the sumo organization is changed to Japan Sumo Association Juridical Foundation. The sumo medical clinic is opened.
1959	January	As the practice of promoting gyoji to elder status is abolished, the names Kimura Shonosuke and Shikimori Inosuke are dropped from the list of elder names.
1960	January	New regulations for gyoji establish a retirement age and limit the number of available positions. The number of tate-gyoji (head referee) is set at two.
	June	The number of per-tournament bouts for rikishi of makushita rank and under is lowered from eight to seven.
1961	January	Retirement ages are established for elders, wakaimonogashira, sewanin, yobidashi, and barbers. (See p.55 for explanation of terms)
1965	January	Tournaments between clans are abolished and those between individuals begun.
1969	May	Video-tape recordings are first used as an aid to settling disputed matches.
	July	Rules are changed to demote ozeki with losing records in two consecutive tournaments to sekiwake. (Provisions are made, however, to reinstate a rikishi if he achieves a winning record in the next tournament.)

Haridashi Information | The "double ring" was so called because there were two rings of bales around the ring, one inside the other. It was referred to as the "bull's eye ring," and the sand between the two rings was called "bull's eye sand."

In 1958, the name of the Japan Grand Sumo Association was changed to the Japan Sumo Association. The methods and regulations of the association changed with the times, gradually evolving into its present form. This section mentions some major events in the history of sumo between the years 1953 and 1993.

| 1971 | May | Rules revised to allow lower-ranked makuuchi rikishi to be paired up with yokozuna and ozeki during tournaments. |

The Kuramae Kokugikan was completed in 1954. The name of the sumo organization was revised to Japan Sumo Association, and many changes in the rules, regulations, and ways of doing things ensued. Sumo became more and more popular as fans tuned in to bouts of Tochinishiki and the first Wakanohana (the Tochi-Waka Era), and then to those of Kashiwado and Taiho (The Haku-Ho Era). With the beginning of live television broadcasts, sumo became a sport accessible to people all over the country.

[New Leaps: 1974 - 1993]

1984	September	The last official tournament is held at the Kuramae Kokugikan. The champion is maegashira Tagaryu.
1985	January	The first official tournament is held at the new Ryogoku Kokugikan.
1988	November	On the last day of the November tournament, yokozuna Onokuni stops yokozuna Chiyonofuji's consecutive-win record at 53. (This is also the final tournament of the Showa Era.)
1989	September	Yokozuna Chiyonofuji receives the National Award of Honor.
1991	September	In order to provide for smoother bouts, fines are instituted for false starts. (See page 39)
1993	March	Akebono Taro is the first non-Japanese to be promoted to the rank of yokozuna.

The rikishi Wajima, Kitanoumi, and Chiyonofuji generated a renewed interest in sumo, and, in 1985, the new Ryogoku Kokugikan was completed. In 1992, with the retirement of grand champion Hokutoumi, grand sumo was without a yokozuna for five straight tournaments. In March 1993, however, American rikishi Akebono was promoted to the top rank, followed by Takanohana in November 1994. These two as well as numerous other powerful young rikishi have ushered in a new era of sumo.

Grand Sumo Operations
The Japan Sumo Association (JSA)

The JSA Organization

The chairman is the chief authority of the JSA. He is elected by his fellow trustees and serves a term of two years. The present chairman is Sakaigawa (the former yokozuna Sadanoyama). who was elected in February 1994.

Supervisors attend meetings of the board of trustees. We can voice opinions but have no voting privileges.

Chairman

The other trustees head various comittees and departments.

mutual election

Board of trustees

Supervisors (3)
Officers of the JSA who take care of its business. They serve terms of two years.

The chairman is elected by the Board of Trustees (10 members including chairman)
These are the leaders of the JSA with the authority to oversee all operations and rule on matters of business. Two-year terms.

Election

Election

The Council
Made up of all qualified elders, four rikishi representatives, and two gyoji. The JSA chairman calls meetings of the council twice a year, and discussion is held concerning various aspects of the association. Elections of trustees and supervisors are held every two years. Only elders are eligible to fill the positions.

The Operations Council
Consists of 22 members, including JSA trustees, elders, rikishi, gyoji, wakaimongashira, sewanin, yobidashi, and barbars, all of whom discuss the JSA from their own perspective in order to make total operations as efficient and smooth as possible.

The council has the final word on all JSA decisions.

Four rikishi reps

Two gyoji reps

Yobidashi (45)

Elders (107)

Rikishi Council

Gyoji (45)

Tokoyama (barbers) (50)

Rikishi Council
All rikishi juryo-level and above are members. The group promotes good interpersonal relations, mutual aid and support, and acts as the voice of rikishi in JSA matters. Meetings are held before every regular tournament. The chairman is usually a top-ranking rikishi.

General employees

Wakaimono-gashira (8)

Sewanin (8)

Haridashi Information

A "one-generation" elder stock is an honor bestowed upon rikishi with outstanding career records. The rikishi serves as an elder under his wrestling name, and his stock is good for one generation only (i.e., he cannot sell his stock to another prospective elder.) Current

The Japan Sumo Association was established to promote and maintain the Japanese national sport, and it runs all aspects of grand sumo. At present there are more than one thousand people under the jurisdiction of the JSA, including elders, rikishi, gyoji, and other employees.

The Yokozuna Judging Committee — *15 member limit*

This board of inquiry was established in 1950. Members include scholars and members of the press knowledgeable in of the sport. The JSA asks this committee to consider candidates for the status of yokozuna.

Operational Judging Committee — *15 member limit*

Established in 1957 as a board of inquiry concerning JSA operational matters. The chairman of the board of trustees calls meetings three times a year before tournaments in Tokyo, and operational problems are discussed. Members include politicians, financiers, and scholars. Terms are two years in length.

Other JSA Positions

Sumo Training School	Trains and educates newly-registered rikishi
Public Relations	Ensures correct communication of all aspects of sumo as the national sport. Promotes sumo scholarship.
Rikishi Lifestyles	Established in 1972 to oversee and handle problems related to the lifestyles of rikishi.
Business	Handles matters related to the Tokyo tournaments (January, May, September), as well as business items not covered by other departments.
Judging	In charge of bout outcomes, bout combinations, and the ranking chart. Committee members (three trustees and twenty others) are elected to one-year terms.
Provincial Tournaments	Handles matters related to tournaments held in Osaka (March), Nagoya (July), and Kyushu (November).
Tours	Takes care of details concerning both domestic and overseas tours.
Sumo Observation Committee	Established in 1972 to prevent intentional losses and other rule infractions.
Occupational Injuries	Makes final decisions, in consultation with the head of the judging committee, on all claims of occupational injury
Mass Media	Press liaison
Security	Handles security at official tournaments.

Other positions include the Sumo Museum Committee, New-apprentice Inspection, Winning Move Committee, and so on. (All data is current as of July 1993)

holders of this title are Taiho and Kitanoumi. (Chiyonofuji – now Kokonoue Oyakata – turned down the honor in favor of a regular position.

A rikishi who spent his life in pursuit of the beauty of sumo

Kasugano Kiyotaka (former yokozuna Tochinishiki)

(1926-1990)

Born Nakata Kiyoshi on February 20, 1926 in Tokyo's Edogawa Ward. His first tournament as a rikishi was January 1939. Nakata was given the nickname "Viper" for the fierce training sessions that carried him to preeminence in his sport. After the September 1954 tournament he was promoted to the rank of yokozuna, the forty-fourth in sumo history. Because of his immense popularity, and that of yokozuna Wakanohana, Tochinishiki's years in the limelight were dubbed the Tochi-Waka Era, felt by many to have been the golden years of post-war sumo. He retired from the sport after the May 1960 tournament, and was given the elder name Kasugano. Along with other powerful JSA positions, he was elected chairman of the board of trustees in January 1974. He served fourteen years, seven terms, in this capacity, a period during which many reforms were made – construction of the new Ryogoku Kokugikan was begun, and improvements were made in the handling of bouts and other operational aspects. Kasugano retired from the position in 1988, turning over the authority to Futagoyama Oyakata (the current Counselor Hanada), but continued to be active in JSA operations, acting as a consultant and head of the Sumo Museum. Mourned by the entire sumo society, he died on January 10, 1990.

The Sumo Life

Kachiage

The Ranking System

Makushita

There are 120 makushita rikishi, ranked 1 through 60, both east and west. Makushita-rank and under compete in seven bouts during each tournament.

Sandanme

200 rikishi hold this position, ranked 1 through 100, east and west. Wrestlers at this level are called "big brother" apprentices (*anideshi*).

Jonidan

There are about 300 rikishi at this level.

Jonokuchi

This is the first step for young sumo apprentices. There is no specific limit on number of rikishi at this rank.

Your life in sumo depends on your rank! If you don't like it, do something about it!!

Th-th-thank you...

Makushita-rank and under wear black mawashi (belts)

Sagari (strands) as limp as yarn

Yokozuna

Ozeki

Sekiwake
Komusubi

Makuuchi

Juryo

(Jumaime)

Makushita

Sandanme

Jonidan

Jonokuchi

Haridashi Information | Any young man who has passed the new-apprentice examination and been registered with the JSA is called rikishi. Wrestlers makushita-rank and under are referred to as rikishi trainees. Juryo and above are called *sekitori*, with treatment differing accordingly.

As of July 1993, there are 920 rikishi in the Japan Sumo Association. These rikishi are divided into ten different ranks and listed on the *banzuke* ranking chart. The ranks form a pyramid, with yokozuna at the top. The treatment each rikishi receives is based solely on his rank, from which fact comes the saying "one position in rank is the difference between heaven and hell."

Yokozuna

In order to attain the pinnacle of sumo, a rikishi must not only have an outstanding record, but also exhibit a combination of physical prowess and strength of character. When an ozeki produces a superior winning record, the Yokozuna Judging Committee is convened to consider promotion. A yokozuna retains his rank until he retires from active participation.

Ozeki

Only outstanding rikishi are promoted to this rank, and approval must be received from the board of trustees.

San'yaku

The ranks of ozeki, sekiwake, and komusubi are referred to as *san'yaku*, or "the three leaders." There are usually two sekiwake and two komusubi, one each for east and west.

Makuuchi

This term refers to all rikishi ranked yokozuna, ozeki, sekiwake, komusubi, and maegashira. There are thirty-two maegashira rikishi, ranked 1 through 16, east and west. All makuuchi rikishi compete for the tournament championship.

Juryo and makuuchi wrestlers have separate ring-entering ceremonies.

All rikishi juryo-rank and above are assigned a lower-rank wrestler as an attendant.

Juryo

There are twenty-six juryo, ranked 1 through 13, east and west. Juryo compete in fifteen bouts during a tournament for the juryo championship. Attaining this rank is a momentous event in the life of a rikishi. He is respectfully referred to as *sekitori*, earns a monthly salary, and is paid incentives based on his win-loss record. He is also eligible to have his hair fashioned in the *oitcho*, or "big ginkgo leaf" style. Life for a juryo wrestler is much different from that of his makushita counterparts.

The "big ginkgo leaf" hair style.

Sagari are made of starched satin.

Sekitori can wear white mawashi (belts) during training sessions.

The kesho-mawashi (decorative loincloth) worn for ring-entering ceremonies.

Banzuke I
How to Read the Ranking Chart

Kannuki

Ranking Chart

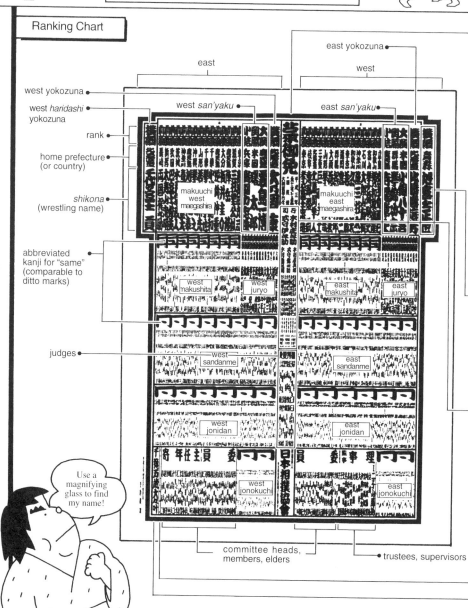

- east yokozuna
- east
- west
- west yokozuna
- west *haridashi* yokozuna
- west *san'yaku*
- east *san'yaku*
- rank
- home prefecture (or country)
- *shikona* (wrestling name)
- makuuchi west maegashira
- makuuchi east maegashira
- abbreviated kanji for "same" (comparable to ditto marks)
- west makushita
- west juryo
- east makushita
- east juryo
- judges
- west sandanme
- east sandanme
- west jonidan
- east jonidan
- west jonokuchi
- east jonokuchi

Use a magnifying glass to find my name!

- committee heads, members, elders
- trustees, supervisors

26

Haridashi Information

The first Nishinoumi was the first rikishi to be listed as a yokozuna on the ranking chart. This was for the May 1890 tournament. The title of yokozuna, however, was not an officially-recognized rank until 1909.

The *banzuke* is the ranking chart that lists the rank and status of all rikishi, gyoji, and elders in the Japan Sumo Association. The banzuke is the absolute rule of sumo society, and the reason why rikishi practice as hard as they do every day.

Gomenkomuru
This formal greeting is left over from the days of benefit sumo. Temples and shrines would begin announcements of upcoming matches with this statement.

How to read the *banzuke*
The name, rank, and home prefecture (or country) of each rikishi is given. Each section is read top to bottom right to left. The first person listed for a given rank has the highest position in it, and the others follow in order. For each position there is an "east" and "west," and the rikishi on the east is considered superior to his west-side counterpart.

East *haridashi* yokozuna
As a rule, there can only be two yokozuna and ozeki each. If there are more, the two in the top positions are *sei* or *regular*, while the others are written in columns that protrude from the *banzuke*, and are referred to as *haridashi*, or "overflow" yokozuna and ozeki.

Gyogi (referees)
The gyogi are also listed by rank, beginning with the top, or *tate-gyoji*, Kimura Shonosuke and Shikimori Inosuke. There are five *gyoji* rankings: *tate-gyoji*, *san'yaku*, makuuchi, juryo, and makushita.

- Announcement that the day's bouts will include pre-sumo with rikishi on both east and west sides.

Senshu Banzai Daidai Kano
This is a statement that expresses hope that there will be no injuries during the tournament and that all seats will be sold out.

Miscellaneous
banzuke Information

Yokozuna-ozeki Rank
The September 1992 tournament was the first one in sixty years that did not include the name of a yokozuna. Officially, there does not have to be a yokozuna, but the *san'yaku* (ozeki, sekiwake, and komusubi) ranks must be filled. For the January 1904 tournament, both ozeki, Hitachiyama and Umegatani, were promoted to yokozuna and the ozeki positions were left empty. To comply with the rules, these two were listed as yokozuna-ozeki.

Yokozuna-ozeki!!

The Brush of the Gyogi
Gyoji write the *banzuke* in a stylized form of writing called *negishi-ryu*. It leaves a minimum of white space on the page and is considered good luck for bringing in a large audience (no spaces left unoccupied). After the gyoji write up the *banzuke*, it is reduced in size and printed at the printing shop run by the JSA. The paper used for the *banzuke* is *ogawa-washi*.

Jonokuchi names are written in a space with a width of 1.7 mm!

Banzuke II
Ranking Decisions and Banzuke Printing

The *Banzuke* Ranking Conference

Banzuke ranking decisions are made soon after a tournament at a conference of all twenty-three judges and observed by the supervisors. The gyoji who runs the meeting records the names of all gyoji and JSA officials, and the names and new ranks of all rikishi on a scroll called *maki*.

All 23 judging committee members

Runs the meeting and records all decisions, but may not give opinions.

Supervisors

gyoji

maki
Used to write up the *banzuke* and schedule bouts for the next tournament.

How Decisions are Made

The record of each rikishi in the tournament just completed is the basis for promotion or demotion. The rule of thumb for makuuchi and juryo ranks is promotion of one position for each win and demotion of one position for each loss.

Final rankings may vary if more than one rikishi ends up in the same position.

If a rikishi is promoted to yokozuna, ozeki, or juryo, the announcement is made immediately because preparations must be made before the next tournament.

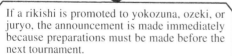

A messenger is sent from the conference to inform the rikishi and his stablemaster of the promotion.

As a new juryo rikishi, I have to order a *kesho mawashi* made!

The completed *maki* is put in the JSA safe until it is time for the banzuke to be announced. No information is allowed to leak out.

Mum's the word!

Top secret!!

28

| Haridashi Information | The *maki* also includes the wins and losses of each rikishi for the last tournament. This is used to pair up matches for the next one. The names of opponents in winning bouts are entered above a rikishi's name, the names of opponents in losing bouts are listed below. |

The new *banzuke* ranks, which can transport a rikishi into either joy or sorrow, are usually settled three days after an official tournament at a banzuke ranking conference attended by all members of the judging committee and supervisors. Discussion begins with the highest-ranked rikishi.

Announcing the New *Banzuke*

The *banzuke* is made public on a Monday at 6 a.m., thirteen days before the next tournament. (In the case of the January tournament, it is announced sixteen days before.) The lower-ranking rikishi from each stable come to collect the printed charts. The example given below is based on the procedure at the Ryogoku Kokugikan.

Rikishi arrive at the hall

JSA employees

I got promoted!

TAXI

Rikishi from nearby stables come on foot with push carts.

At 6 a.m., the Kokugikan east dressing room is opened, and the rikishi file in to pick up the wrapped packages. The room is filled with the smell of printing ink.

The packages are set out, labeled for individual stables.

Entrance

The rikishi sent are usually those who are most likely to be promoted on the new *banzuke*.

About twenty days before the *banzuke* is announced, the *maki* is given to the gyoji who will write it up. It takes him about ten days to complete the job.

The gyoji uses calligraphy ink on a piece of kent paper 108 cm x 78 cm.

I write up the original in an isolated room.

The printed *banzuke* measures 57.5 cm x 43.8 cm.

The original is then taken to the sumo printing shop where it is printed up in guarded secrecy.

Approximately 400,000 copies are printed. The number varies from tournament to tournament.

Offset printing

The Examination for New Apprentices

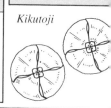

Regulations

All young men who want to become rikishi must be admitted to a stable. The rules are: young men aged 15 to 23 who have completed compulsory education. Must be at least 173 cm tall and weigh a minimum of 75 kg.

men aged 15 to 23

173 cm and over

75 kg or more

Starting Out at Makushita

Some rikishi aged 20 to 25 who have wrestled in college or on a company team start their rikishi careers at the rank of makushita.

The stablemaster who has recruited a young man will send in the application for the new-apprentice examination. The application must also include a parental consent form, a copy of the family register, and a medical examination record.

Japan Sumo Association

Entrance to the World of Sumo

A stable-master must submit the application

Examination application

Hello!

Stable

Stablemaster

Application form

Parental consent form

Family register

Doctor's report

How Non-Japanese are Accepted

If a citizen of a country other than Japan wishes to enter a sumo stable, he must have two sponsors and an elder (stablemaster) to vouch for him before he can go through the examination.

Sumo

Two sponsors of good reputation

Haridashi Information Usually a large number of prospective rikishi apply before the March tournament, about the time the school year ends. Celebrations are held throughout the tournament as the new apprentices achieve the number of wins required to qualify for *banzuke* ranking.

Future yokozuna and ozeki gather for the new-apprentice examination five days before each official tournament. After passing the examination, the new rikishi are registered with the JSA and participate in their first tournament bout.

The New-Apprentice Examination

The examination is held several days before a tournament. Each young man is weighed, measured, and given a physical exam under the watchful eye of the chairman and co-chairman of the judging committee. The March examination, which takes place right after school graduations, is always the busiest. In 1992, of 160 young men who were examined 151 were passed.

Some boys fill up on potatoes and water just before the exam. They must weigh 75 kg only for the few moments they are on the scale.

OK, that's 75 kg.

Tokyo exams take place at the Kokugikan

Height and Weight Exam

First comes the height test. The chairman and co-chairman of the judging committee keep a close eye on proceedings.

Next comes the physical exam administered by a JSA doctor.

Ouch!

Blood is taken for various tests

Look at that! He lifted his heels when nobody was watching!

Pass!

If a young man passes the exam, he is registered with the JSA and recognized as a rikishi.

Even then, a third of all new apprentices quit within a year.

Rikishi!!

Jonokuchi and Jonidan
From Pre-sumo to Jonokuchi and Jonidan

A new apprentice has six months toget three pre-sumo wins.

maezumo

The apprentices are divided into east and west and their names are written on a scroll (*maki*). Match combinations are made and wins and losses recorded.

New apprentices begin competition from the second day of a tournament as *maezumo* (pre-sumo) rikishi and are not listed on the *banzuke*. They are officially ranked as "new" jonokuchi (*shinjo*) as soon as they win three bouts of *maezumo*.

Young gyoji take turns refereeing the bouts.

Apprentices sit around the ring and wait for their names to be called,.

Three wins

Shinjo Celebration

Announcements are usually made on the middle (eighth) day of a tournament during a break in sandanme bouts. The wrestlers then become jonokuchi rikishi and their names appear on the *banzuke* for the next tournament.

Teuchi Ceremony

At the end of the last day of a tournament, the newly-promoted jonokuchi rikishi come up to the ring, drink sake, and clap in the direction of the yobidashi. This is the official close of the tournament.

New gyoji apprentice

Wakaimonogashira judges, and yobidash also participate.

Shinjo rikishi borrow *kesho mawashi* from their stablemaster or *sekitori* stablemates to wear for the ceremony.

I'm a *shinjo*!

Receiving a Wrestling Name (*shikona*)

A *shinjo* usually receives his wrestling name from his stablemaster or sometimes a stable supporter. Wrestlers with the same first and last names, are often given *shikona* for pre-sumo in order to avoid confusion.

My name is Yamamoto Norio!

Same names!

Haridashi Information

All rikishi makushita and under are "rikishi trainees." They receive allowances and travel money for each tournament. Travel money usually comes in the form of train tickets to the tournament hall.

A new apprentice passes his examination, and then begins pre-sumo competition on the second day of the tournament. After three wins he is promoted to jonokuchi, under which rank he will compete in the next official tournament. This section follows new wrestlers from *maezumo* (pre-sumo) through to the jonidan rank.

Jonidan

Jonidan is the fourth level on the ranking chart. In other words, second from the bottom. There are currently 390 jonidan rikishi.

Jonidan Tournament Championship 200,000 yen.

Tournament allowance 75,000 yen

Incentive money *1500 yen per win *3500 per win from the fourth win

Mawashi (belt) wrapped in a scarf (*furoshiki*)

Jonokuchi and jonidan wear only yukata

"Elder brothers" to new trainees

Young rikishi, especially jonokuchi and jonidan, are called *toriteki.*

Another name we have is "underwear bearer...."

heap crepe ash

Bare feet and wooden sandals all year round

The strands on the belts of lower-ranked rikishi are sparse and limp.

Jonokuchi

Jonokuchi is the fifth – the lowest – rank on the *banzuke*. This is the beginning of the long professional life of a sumo wrestler.

Jonokuchi Tournament championship 100,000 yen

Tournament allowance 70,000 yen

Incentives * 1500 per win *3500 per win from the fourth win

This is what we wear!

Stables supply cotton yukata for warm-weather months and thin wool kimono for winter.

I always eat last. Cold rice for every meal....

My name is here some-where...

Cheap crepe sash

The same mawashi belt for tournaments and practice

Sturdy wooden geta and bare feet

33

The Sumo Training School
A Day in the Life of an Apprentice Rikishi

Combs

Training Session

Training is aimed at teaching young rikishi the basics of sumo as well as instilling in him the mental and physical stamina to endure fierce practice sessions, which are called *keiko*. Elders and higher-ranked rikishi supervise the training, which lasts from 7 to 10 o'clock each morning.

The training school is on the second floor of one of the buildings attached to the Kokugikan.

Mandatory training lasts six months

Late again!

Learning to stamp (*shiko*)

This builds up my lower body and strengthens my back and legs.

Entrance

This room can and does hold 130 wrestlers. When it becomes too full, groups are divided up to work on individual techniques.

Raised tatami mats for observers

Illustration of the Sumo Training School

Name of rikishi and stable

Toilet & bath

Technique is taught by four elders and makushita rikishi

This builds up my upper body and strengthens my arms. I learn how to pace.

Three practice rings

Keiko gym

Shinto shrine

Steel pillar

Steel pillars

A large frame holds the characters (*renma*), or "training."

Next!!

The basics of pushing

Trainees read out their motto in unison after practice

Steel pillars

I learn how to receive blows to avoid injury

Training policy
1. Good manners are the core of a rikishi's character
2. A trainee practices in strict accordance with the teachings of his elders
3. A trainee always dresses properly and keeps himself clean

Attack (*butsukari*)

Ring ceremonies

We learn how to bow, do *chirichozu* and other ceremonial motions

Classes are held from a week after regular tournaments until a few days before the next banzuke is announced. Training is halted during tournaments.

College sumo wrestlers are exempted from training sessions

They only attend classroom courses

Haridashi Information The first group of trainees were inducted at the September 1957 tournament. The first graduate to become a yokozuna was Tamanoumi (first tournament March 1959, the tenth class of trainees).

New apprentices who pass the initial examination spend the next six months at the Sumo Training School, established in 1957, where they learn wrestling basics and get the classroom learning required of all rikishi. This section describes what new rikishi do during a typical day at the school.

Classes

Trainees go straight from their training into the classroom. Professionals in their respective fields are invited to give lectures.

University professors teach many of the classes

I guess they need the extra sleep....

Everyone attends

Photos of all of the stablemasters are displayed in the back of the classroom so that apprentices can become familiar with them.

Entrance

Two rikishi occupy each desk. It is a tight squeeze

Blackboard

Classroom

Photos of the instructors and all past schoolmasters

Trainees dress in yukata for class

Faculty office

Classes end about noon. Trainees bathe at the school and take their first meal of the day in the dining hall in the basement of the Kokugikan. After their meal, they take a nap, make sure they are dressed neatly, and then return to their stables.

The first meal of the day. Rikishi often have five or six bowls of rice. This is also one of the few breaks apprentices get during the day.

Let's eat!

Now it's back to the stable to run errands!

Sumo History — Trainees learn the history of sumo in Japan and its role as the national sport.

Sports Medicine — How to avoid injury and take care of cuts, etc. to avoid infection.

Social Studies — Learning to function as an adult member of society. (Common sense / Knowledge)

Calligraphy — Calligraphy is used for spiritual training

Biology — Correct comprehension of the human body and how it works, especially as concerns sports.

Shigin — Trainees learn this traditional form of singing with an eye towards spiritual development.

Sandanme and Makushita

Makushita	The highest of the unsalaried ranks. There are 120 makushita rikishi, numbered 1 through 60, east and west.

Makushita championship 500,000 yen

Tournament allowance 120,000 yen

2500 yen per win
600 yen per win after achieving a winning record *(kachi koshi)*

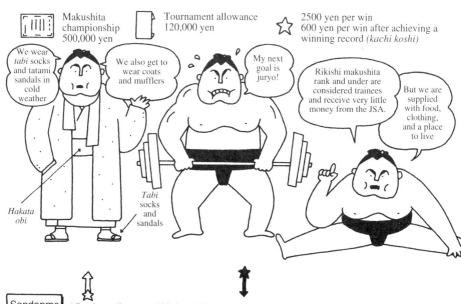

We wear *tabi* socks and tatami sandals in cold weather

We also get to wear coats and mufflers

My next goal is juryo!

Rikishi makushita rank and under are considered trainees and receive very little money from the JSA.

But we are supplied with food, clothing, and a place to live

Hakata obi

Tabi socks and sandals

Sandanme	"Sandanme" means "third rank." There are 200 sandanme rikishi in all, 100 each, east and west.

Sandanme championship 300,000 yen

Tournament allowance 80,000 yen

Incentives
2000 yen per win
4500 yen per win after achieving a winning record *(kachi-koshi)*

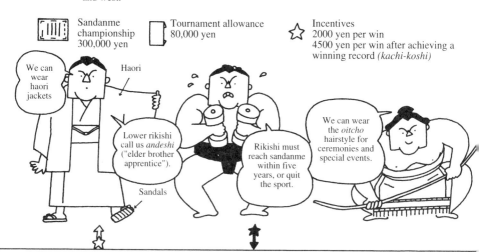

We can wear haori jackets

Haori

Lower rikishi call us *andeshi* ("elder brother apprentice").

Rikishi must reach sandanme within five years, or quit the sport.

We can wear the *oitcho* hairstyle for ceremonies and special events.

Sandals

Haridashi Information	Sandanme wrestlers can wear haori jackets and softer sandals. The real tatami sandals, however, are not allowed until makushita.

Wrestlers makushita rank and under are referred to as "sumo trainees." Treatment of these apprentices is a far cry from that received by *sekitori* who are juryo rank and above. Attaining the status of *sekitori* is the drive behind the spartan lives these rikishi lead.

College Grads Start Out at Makushita

New wrestlers who have excellent college sumo records or who have excelled in a corporate-sponsored league may be allowed by the JSA to make their debut in the lowest makushita position. As of January 1993, men aged 20 to 25 who have achieved a certain record at required amateur tournaments are also eligible. These rikishi are not required to meet height or weight requirements.

Should I become a makushita rikishi...

...or get a more conventional job?

I'm a pretty smart guy

Sumo · Rest of Society

Standard Amateur Tournaments and Records
(All records must have been achieved within two years of JSA registration)

Tournament	Record
All Japan Title	A top-16 wrestler
National Student Title Kokutai Adult A All Japan Non-professional Team Title	One championship or two second or third places

The Glamorous "Big Ginkgo Leaf"
Sandanme rikishi wear the Big Ginkgo Leaf *(oitcho)* hairstyle for the bow-twirling ceremony and other special events. Makushita rikishi do their hair this way when scheduled to wrestle a juryo opponent.

After I meet a juryo opponent, I have to go back to the old *chonmage* topknot style.

A baby ginkgo leaf

Juryo

Juryo

On the *banzuke* chart, juryo (official name is *jumaime*) is written on the second section from the top. It is in the same section as makushita, but names are written in thicker characters in order to make a distinction. The origin of the name of this rank comes from the Edo Era, when the top ten makushita positions were paid a salary of ten *ryo* (juryo). There are now twenty-six juryo positions, numbered 1 through 13, east and west.

 Juryo Championship 2 million yen

 Salary (before taxes) 870,000 yen

Incentives Paid based on the salary of each wrestler. The lowest figure a juryo receives per tournament is 100,000 yen.

Travel Expenses Lodging 5,000 yen, Per diem 1,200 yen

Call me *sekitori*

The Big Ginkgo Leaf *(oitcho)*

I can wear a formal outfit carrying my family crest, and I get a lower-ranked rikishi to carry my bags and run errands!

Errand boys are makushita rank and lower

I can wear a white cotton mawashi for practicing

Neatly-starched strands

This satin mawashi is for tournaments

38

Haridashi Information

The head judge will inform the chairman of the JSA board of trustees if he suspects a rikishi of deliberately stalling the beginning of a bout. The chairman then fines the rikishi in question.

A rikishi has finally arrived when he is promoted to juryo. He is called *sekitori*, a term of respect, receives a salary, has his hair done in the Big Ginkgo Leaf style, is assigned an errand boy, and so on. In short, the treatment he is given is a far cry from that of a makushita wrestler. This section gives a glimpse of the more glamorous side of sumo.

I compete in fifteen bouts per tournament.

Lower ranks only have seven.

If I intentionally stall a bout, I will be fined 50,000 yen.

Only juryo ranks and above use the strength water and paper and get to toss salt into the ring.

Ready!! Juryo have three minutes in-ring pre-bout time, makushita and under have two minutes.

I wear my *kesho-mawashi* apron for the juryo ring entering ceremony.

And I'm the one who carries it for him!

Juryo use a lacquered wicker trunk (*akeni*) to carry their *kesho mawashi*, mawashi, and other accessories to the tournament hall.

The apron weighs more than 10 kg and costs upward of one million yen.

akeni

39

Geta

Makuuchi

Makuuchi

All of the wrestlers in the top section of the *banzuke* ranking chart are makuuchi. The yokozuna are listed on the right, followed, on the east and west sides, by *san'yaku* and maegashira rikishi. Varying sizes of letters indicate the changes in rank. There are thirty maegashira rikishi all together, numbered 1 through 15, east and west.

Makuuchi Championship is 10 million yen

Salary 1,099,000 yen

Incentives
Paid based on the salary of each wrestler. The lowest figure a makuuchi rikishi (except yokozuna and ozeki) receives per tournament is 150,000 yen.

The "Three Awards" *(sansho)* for excellent tournament performance
The Technique Award, the Fighting Spirit Award and the Outstanding Performance Award are 2 million yen each.

Bout incentive prizes 60,000 each (of which rikishi receive 30,000)

Travel Allowances
Lodging 5700 yen
Per diem 1400 yen

For tournaments outside of Tokyo, rikishi receive thirty-five days worth of travel allowance.

Makuuchi

Sekitori wear a formal kimono with a family crest *(montsuki)* and *hakama* trousers

In-ring pre-bout times is four minutes

The fine for stalling a bout *(matta)* is 100,000 yen

The belts of sekitori are officially limited to black, purple, and navy blue, but they actually wear a wide variety of colors which the JSA has tacitly accepted.

Haridashi Information Makuuchi and lower rikishi take care of the needs of *sekitori*. Juryo wrestlers each have one or two assigned to them. Makuuchi have two to five, and a yokozuna may have ten or more.

Maegashira make up the largest group of top-ranked rikishi. Also known as *hiramaku*, they wrestle each other, yokozuna and *san'yaku* for the makuuchi championship.

The Maegashira Ring-entering Ceremony

Held after the completion of all juryo bouts. The ceremony is carried out very much as it has been historically, but in a somewhat shorter version due to the increase in the number of rikishi.

The rikishi come down the *hanamichi* (road of flowers) that leads to the ring. They are led by the gyoji in ascending order of rank. The east side comes down the eastern aisle and the west side from the west.

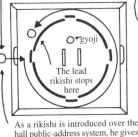

The lead rikishi stops here

On odd days, the ceremony is led by the east, on even days by the west.

Same order as the juryo ceremony

After the ceremony is completed, the rikishi leave the ring in the same order returning the way they came.

As a rikishi is introduced over the hall public-address system, he gives a bow and climbs up into the ring

Rikishi go around the ring, maintaining a perfect circle by walking with one foot on either side of the bales describing the ring.

① Stand with back to inside of ring
② Turn towards the inside
③ Clap once to show one is unarmed
④ Hold up one arm, and
⑤ Lift apron with both hands to symbolize stance and stamping
⑥ Hold up both arms to symbolize end of stamping

Gold Star

A gold star is given to a maegashira wrestler in recognition of a win against a yokozuna. For every gold star he achieves, a rikishi receives 25,000 yen per tournament for the rest of his career. (see p.71) As of July 1997, the rikishi who has the record number of gold stars is the current Akinoshima with fifteen. The total prize money for this feat comes to 375,000 per tournament.

San'yaku I
Komusubi and Sekiwake

Incentive prizes

San'yaku   Tournament awards are the same as for all makuuchi rikishi.

 Salary
1,421,000 yen

 Special bonus
50,000 yen

Travel Allowance
Lodging 6500 yen
Per diem 1600 yen

Paid to *san'yaku* and above for every tournament in which they compete at least eleven days. They receive two-thirds of this figure for up to ten days participation, one-third for up to five days, and none at all for missing an entire tournament.

San'yaku wrestlers do not receive gold stars for beating a yokozuna

Komusubi

A losing-record (*make-koshi*) for one tournament means demotion to maegashira

Kensho : Incentive Prizes

Kensho are special incentive prizes offered for winners of individual bouts. The cost to sponsor a *kensho* is 60,000 yen, and any number of sponsors can offer a prize for any makuuchi bout. For each prize offered, the winner gets 30,000 yen. The JSA takes 25,000 yen to cover any income tax the winner may be liable for, and 5000 yen goes for the cost of the advertising banner and announcement over the public-address system. If a bout is won by forfeit or if it is declared a draw, the money is returned to the sponsors. As of this writing, the record number of *kensho* placed on a single bout was twenty-six for a 1964 bout between Taiho and Tochinoumi.

Haridashi Information On the last day of a tournament, the winners of the final bouts receive one of the following three prizes from the gyoji: bow strings, a bow, and an arrow. These represent, in order, "the desire of a komusubi," the "desire of a sekiwake," and "the desire of an ozeki."

San'yaku, the "three positions," refer to the ozeki, sekiwake, and komusubi-ranked rikishi. Currently, however, it frequently refers only to the komusubi and sekiwake. There must be at least one sekiwake and komusubi for both east and west sides, for a total of four.

A sekiwake's record for the last three tournaments is the basis for promotion to ozeki.

Wins	Losses
11	4
10	5

San'yaku zoroifumi "*San'yaku* Assembly"

This ceremony is held before the final three bouts of the last day of a tournament by the top three non-yokozuna rikishi on each side. Participants are usually the competitors in those last three bouts.

43

San'yaku II
Ozeki

Promotion to Ozeki

I ask the board of trustees to attend a meeting

Head of the Judging Committee

After a sekiwake has three straight tournaments with strong winning records, the head of the Judging Committee asks the board of trustees to assemble.

Three good tournaments

Back to square one

Not approved

The board of trustees discusses whether the rikishi should be promoted.

Approved

Banzuke Ranking Conference

The rule of thumb is a total of 33 wins over three tournaments.

A new ozeki is born

As soon as the decision is made, a messenger is sent from the JSA

The news of the promotion is formally relayed to the rikishi and his stablemaster.

You have been promoted to ozeki.

I humbly accept this honor and will do my best to uphold the title of ozeki.

New ozeki

Stab masi and wife

44

The ozeki with the longest career in that position was Takanohana (father of the yokozuna with the same name), with fifty tournaments. This record is followed by Hokuten'yu (Hitachiyama *oyakata*) forty-four tournaments, and Konishiki with thirty-seven tournaments.

Ozeki is the highest of the *san'yaku* ranks, with only yokozuna above it. As with sekiwake and komusubi, there must be at least one rikishi ranked ozeki on both east and west sides. If there is no ozeki, a yokozuna will fill the spot under the title of yokozuna-ozeki.

Ozeki

Tournament champions and incentive money (*kensho*) are the same as for other makuuchi rikishi. (see p.40)

Salary
1,971,000 yen

Tournament Allowance
150,000 yen

Incentive Money (see p.72)
Paid each tournament based on the total number of career wins. The minimum amount for an ozeki is 250,000 yen.

Travel Allowance (see p. 40)
Lodging 7500 yen
Per diem 2000 yen

New ozeki receive a sum of 500,000 in honor of their promotion

Ozeki are demoted after two consecutive losing tournaments

My next goal is yokozuna

To be promoted to yokozuna I have to win two tournaments in a row or have a record equal to it.

Ozeki privileges

Rikishi ranked sekiwake and below face demotion after any tournament in which they have one losing record. Ozeki, on the other hand, are allowed to have a losing tournament. An ozeki who has sat out a tournament or who has a losing record is referred to as *kadoban*, or "keeper of the corner" (the word alone has a precarious sound to it). If the losing streak extends to a second tournament, the ozeki is demoted to sekiwake. There is, however, one more loophole: if the rikishi gets ten wins or more in the tournament immediately following demotion, he can return to his ozeki position.

Oooh... I can't lose the next one!

One losing record

Yokozuna I
Promotion to Yokozuna

Kokugikan Hall

Yokozuna Promotion

Two consecutive tournament championships

Ozeki

When an ozeki wins two straight tournaments or achieves a similarly excellent record, the JSA asks the Yokozuna Judging committee to convene to discuss promotion.

Dignity

Power

Consultation

Start all over again

Few yokozuna have actually won two consecutive tournaments as ozeki.

Not approved

Yokozuna Judging Committee

This comittee is formed by JSA advisers, who discuss the promotion and submit a report to the JSA.

The decision must be unanimous

Approved

There are twelve committee members

A tournament may end with several rikishi meeting in a playoff for the championship. A playoff bouts is not included in the official win-loss record.

Haridashi Information

Yokozuna are numbered as they are promoted. If more than one rikishi is promoted at the same time, they are not assigned numbers until they retire, with the first to retire receiving the smaller number.

Yokozuna is the pinnacle of a sumo career. A rikishi is required to have not only a superior record, but also a certain dignity and strength of character. Since 1927, only thirty-four rikishi have been promoted to yokozuna, beginning with Tamanishiki (no. 32) in 1932. Takanohana, promoted in November 1994, is yokozuna no. 65. Read on to learn how an ozeki makes the final step to yokozuna.

Board of Trustees
At the JSA, the board of trustees is assembled, and the recommendation of the Yokozuna Judging Committee is considered.

Banzuke Ranking Conference
After the board of trustees gives its approval, the Banzuke Ranking Conference is held and the promotion is formally completed.

"Communication Ceremony"
A messenger from the JSA delivers the news of promotion to the rikishi and his stablemaster

You have been promoted to yokozuna by unanimous vote of the Banzuke Ranking Conference.

I humbly accept the decision and will do my best to uphold the honor of the title of yokozuna.

Yokozuna!

The ultimate goal of all rikishi

A yokozuna is never demoted. He maintains his rank until he retires

The Yoshida Family and the Yokozuna License
The Yoshida Tsukasa family formalized the role of yokozuna, originally as a part of the Shinto ground-breaking ceremony, and created the basis for the present yokozuna system. Until 1951, the Yoshida family in Kyushu issued the license for every new yokozuna. In 1951, the JSA began to issue licenses independently.

This license makes me a yokozuna.

47

Yokozuna II
Yokozuna Conpensation and Rituals

Gohei

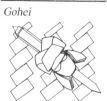

Yokozuna

Championship awards and kensho incentive prizes are the same as for makuuchi wrestlers (see p.40).

Salary
2,369,000 yen

Tournament Allowance (see p. 42) 200,000 yen

Incentive Money
Paid each tournament based on the total number of career wins. The minimum amount for a yokozuna is 375,000 yen.

The Yokozuna rope is 4m long and weighs about 15kg. At its thickest point it is 15cm in diameter.

Shiranui Style has two loops in the bow

Making the Rope (*Tsunauchi* Ceremony)
As soon as promotion is announced, all the stablemates of the new yokozuna prepare to make the ceremonial rope. With everyone working, it takes two to three hours to complete, and a new one is made before every official tournament held in Tokyo.

One! Two ! Three!

A thick column

All of the rikishi in the stable are present. The actual work is done by juryo-rank wrestlers and above, but the lower-ranked men beat drums and cheer the others on.

Red and white headband symbolizes a celebratory event

A copper wire is at the center of the rope. Three ropes are made of soft linen wrapped in stiffer cotton and then twisted to the left.

Five sacred paper strands (*shide*) are attached

White gloves

Rikishi wear white cotton aprons over their mawashi

Haridashi Information
The three-stage stance (*sandan-gamae*), a basic sumo position, is performed by East and West yokozuna on occasions of extreme importance, such as the opening of a new Kokugikan Hall.

After a yokozuna is promoted, his stablemates make the ceremonial rope (also called *yokozuna*) for him, and more experienced yokozuna teach him how to perform the ring-entering ceremony which he performs at Meiji Jingu Shrine in Tokyo, his first appearance in his new position.

Travel Allowance
Lodging 8000 yen
Per diem   3000 yen

A new yokozuna receives one million yen in honor of his promotion.

The JSA pays for the cost of making the ceremonial rope.

Yokozuna Promotion Ceremony
Usually held six days after the final day of the last tournament, this is the occasion when the chairman of the board of trustees gives the new yokozuna his license. After receiving it, he performs his first yokozuna ring-entering ceremony in the courtyard of the famous Meiji Jingu shrine.

The yokozuna receives his license and yokozuna rope after receiving Shinto purification

Unryu style has one loop in the rope.

The yokozuna and his stablemaster make the final decision of either *shiranui* or *unryu* style, but they listen carefully to the opinions of others before doing so.

This is my first ring-entering ceremony

Yokozuna III
Yokozuna Ring-entering Ceremony

The gyoji leads the way followed by the herald, yokozuna, and sword bearer

opposite front

The Yokozuna Ring Entering Ceremony

In the case of the east yokozuna

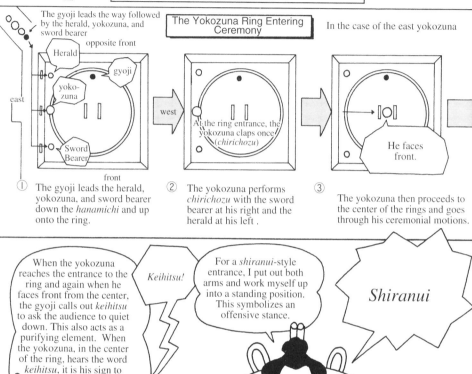

Herald

gyoji

yoko-zuna

east

Sword Bearer

front

At the ring entrance, the yokozuna claps once (*chirichozu*)

west

He faces front.

① The gyoji leads the herald, yokozuna, and sword bearer down the *hanamichi* and up onto the ring.

② The yokozuna performs *chirichozu* with the sword bearer at his right and the herald at his left .

③ The yokozuna then proceeds to the center of the rings and goes through his ceremonial motions.

When the yokozuna reaches the entrance to the ring and again when he faces front from the center, the gyoji calls out *keihitsu* to ask the audience to quiet down. This also acts as a purifying element. When the yokozuna, in the center of the ring, hears the word *keihitsu*, it is his sign to begin the ceremonial motions.

Keihitsu!

For a *shiranui*-style entrance, I put out both arms and work myself up into a standing position. This symbolizes an offensive stance.

Shiranui

The sword bearer carries the sword in his right hand.

Haridashi Information The sword bearer and herald are usually makuuchi wrestlers from the same clan as the yokozuna. When a yokozuna retires from active competition, he his accompanied by ozeki or yokozuna from his clan for his final ring-entering ceremony.

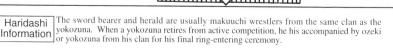

There are two types of yokozuna ring-entering ceremonies, *unryu* and *shiranui*. Differences include the way the yokozuna rope is tied and motions during the ring-entering ceremony.

The party leaves the ring.

The yokozuna enters the ring after the makuuchi wrestlers have completed their bouts. On odd days the east yokozuna goes first, and on even days the west yokozuna takes the lead.

The gyoji always leads off

Step back to entrance

④ The yokozuna returns to the entrance and performs *chirichozu* again.

⑤ The yokozuna leaves the ring, this time led by the herald and followed by the sword bearer and gyoji.

Unryu

I put my left arm at my side, spread my right arm straight out, and work myself up into a standing position. The left arm symbolizes defense, and the right arm offense.

The herald clears the way for the yokozuna.

The herald is usually of a lower rank than the sword bearer.

Retirement Sumo and the Haircutting Ceremony

Retirement A rikishi and his stablemaster decide when he will retire. After the decision is made, they notify the JSA.

You've done a good job

I'm losing my strength....

The stablemaster and rikishi decide when it is time to retire.

I submit notice of the decision to the JSA

The JSA accepts it

The Japan Sumo Association

Now I start making announcements to my support groups and begin planning my retirement sumo event.

"Retirement sumo" is generally limited to rikishi who have competed as *sekitori* (juryo or higher) for at least thirty tournaments.

When a rikishi retires, a hair-cutting ceremony (*danpatsu-shiki*) is held. This is an occasion when makushita-ranked and lower rikishi can tie their hair in the *oitcho* style. When a rikishi follows retirement by taking up a position as a JSA elder it is called *intai*, or simply "retirement." If he is leaving sumo permanently, it is called *haigyo*, or "abandoning the profession."

You've been a fighter....

Haridashi Information The *mage* topknot is the symbol of the sumo wrestler. When a rikishi retires and has his topknot cut off, he will often keep it in a glass case as a reminder of his years in the sport.

In the results-oriented world of sumo, even the greatest rikishi have to retire. The JSA rules state that a rikishi who has completed 30 tournaments as a sekitori may hold a retirement sumo event. This event brings to a close a rikishi's career in the ring.

Retirement Sumo

Retirement sumo is usually held after a Tokyo tournament at the Ryogoku Kokugikan. The retiring rikishi holds a hair-cutting ceremony and starts out on the his "second career."

Retirement Sumo includes a variety of events.

My last ring-entering ceremony

Leaders of society, supporters, brother rikishi, and stablemasters all take turns.

Haircutting ceremony

We only cut a few hairs.

Rikishi representatives wear mawashi

Special JSA scissors are used

The stablemaster goes last, and cuts off the whole topknot.

Scissors

A new start!

A Second Career

Three-stage stance (top)

Retired rikishi

I'll start my second career here.

Have you elder stock?

YES ➡

A yokozuna can work as a non-stockholding elder for five years under his wrestling name. If he doesn't buy stock within that time, he must leave the profession.

Special privilege for yokozuna

NO ⬇

A completely different career.

Chanko restaurant!

Businessman …

…or teacher

The family business

Continue working for the JSA

YES ➡

A rikishi may stay on at his stable as a "manager." Not an official JSA employee, the stablemaster pays his salary out of his own pocket money.

NO ⬇

Leave Sumo

The right-hand-man of my *oyakata*

Haridashi Information | Rikishi receive a form of severance pay, the figure depends upon rank and number of career bouts. Yokozuna, ozeki, and elders receive an additional lump sum at retirement.

After retirement from active competition, a rikishi can stay in the employ of the JSA if he owns "elder" stock. There are also other special positions, such as *wakaimonogashira* and *sewanin*, but otherwise a rikishi will have to leave sumo all together and pursue a career in mainstream society.

Elders

There are 105 positions for elder stockholders, and they are all full!!

The asking price for elder stock is reported to be 15 to 20 billion yen.

Mandatory retirement age is 65

A rikishi must register himself as an elder immediately upon retirement

There are 105 elders in the JSA as well as two one-generation positions held by Taiho and Kitanoumi, for a total of 107. A rikishi must own stock before he retires so that he can register himself as an elder as soon as he gives up active competition. Requirements for purchasing stock when one becomes available are Japanese citizenship, one complete tournament at a makuuchi rank or twenty consecutive tournaments/twenty-five total tournaments at juryo.

son

Conditions are waived if a son passes stock on to his son.

Originally, stock was passed on (not sold) if a rikishi would agree to look after his predecessor.

father

Wakaimonogashira
(head of the youth)

This is a position held by retired rikishi who did not manage to achieve the rank of juryo. The stablemaster applies to the JSA, and the board of trustees hires him. A *wakaimonogashira* is paid by the JSA, but works for his own stable. He looks after and helps train lower-rank wrestlers. He also keeps track of wrestling records, supervises new apprentices, makes sure their training program runs smoothly, and so on. Wakaimonogashira play an important backstage role in the operations of grand sumo.

Only eight men can hold this position

Mandatory retirement age is 65

Recently, some have had experience in makuuchi ranks.

Sewanin
(assistants)

As with *wakaimonogashira*, rikishi who retire at the makushita rank have their stablemasters apply for the position to the board of trustees. *Sewanin* act as property managers as well as assistants to *wakaimonogashira*.

There are only eight positions and they are all full now.

Retirement at age 65

There is no established job description. *Sewanin* work for the JSA and for individual stables, taking care of any and all odd jobs.

"Devil of the Ring"

Hanada Katsuji (formerly yokozuna Wakanohana)

Born March 16, 1928 in Hirosaki, Aomori Prefecture, Hanada made his sumo debut during the November 1946 tournament as the first Wakanohana, and became the forty-fifth yokozuna directly following the January 1958 tournament. His vigorous combatant style and heroic moves earned him the nickname "Devil of the Ring." After his retirement in 1962, he broke off from the Hanakago stable and formed the Futagoyama stable. In 1988 he succeeded Kasugano as the JSA chairman, continuing his predecessor's efforts to impose sanctions on intentional bout stalling and forfeiture by introducing a system of monetary fines. He retired from the chairmanship in February 1993 and from the JSA in March 1994. At that time, he entrusted the Futagoyama stable to his brother Fujishima oyakata (formerly ozeki Takanohana), creating one of the strongest stables in sumo history. Currently, Hanada serves as a counselor to the JSA and head of the Sumo Museum. His study of sumo history takes him on trips around the world.

The Sumo Stable

The Sumo Stable

Three-stage stance (lower)

Establishing a Sumo Stable

When an elder decides that he wants to start his own stable, he must have the permission of his pre-retirement *oyakata* and the JSA board of trustees.

On my own!

Approval

The Japan Sumo Association

Permission

Stablemaster

Conditions for Establishing a Stable

Training room (stable)

Elder stock

I'm an Elder

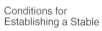

Rikishi

At least 2

Finally!! I'm an oyakata with my own stable!

Stable Organization (an example)

Stablemaster (*oyakata*)

His wife (*okami-san*) Mother to rikishi, budget balancer, and loyal wife!

yobidashi

sekitori

Manager (right-hand man of the *oyakata*)

gyoji

Barber

rikishi makushita-rank and under

Our Stable

Haridashi Information | Tournament competition is between stables. No rikishi wrestles against a stablemate. In years past there have been other systems such as competition between east and west and between clans (*ichimon*).

The sumo stable (*beya*) is the foundation of sumo society. All rikishi belong to a stable. Only elders who own elder stock and can meet a few minimum conditions are allowed to run stables and train rikishi.

Running a Sumo Stable

A stablemaster is paid a salary by the JSA. The JSA provides maintenance funds and various other benefits. These funds are used to run a *beya*.

The goal of every stable is to produce a *sekitori*.

Besides the glory, a *sekitori* can also mean the difference between poverty and prosperity.

Support Funds
Paid to stablemasters each tournament for each rikishi:

Yokozuna	300,000 yen
Ozeki	200,000 yen
San'yaku	100,000 yen
Maegashira	50,000 yen
Juryo	30,000 yen

Sekitori

Rikishi Training Funds
The JSA pays 60,000 yen a month per rikishi trainee (makushita rank and under) in each stable.

Training Room Maintenance
The JSA pays stablemasters a certain amount per month per rikishi (based on rikishi rank) for upkeep of the stable training room. The board of trustees decides how much will be paid out, but refuses to disclose the actual sum.

Stable Maintenance
Support funds, also undisclosed, paid out based on the number of rikishi trainees.

This is where I come in

The budget master

Stables without any *sekitori* often operate in the red

Competition by stable
The current system of competition by stable was introduced in January 1965. During official tournaments, a rikishi will never compete against a stablemate. The only exception to this rule is a championship playoff where stablemates are tied for the title.

Stable A

Stable B

Hakkeyoi!

The Stable Training Room (keiko-jo) Illustrated

The training room (keiko-jo) in each stable is located on the ground floor of the building, and has one or two rings. The illustrations below are an example of such a training room.

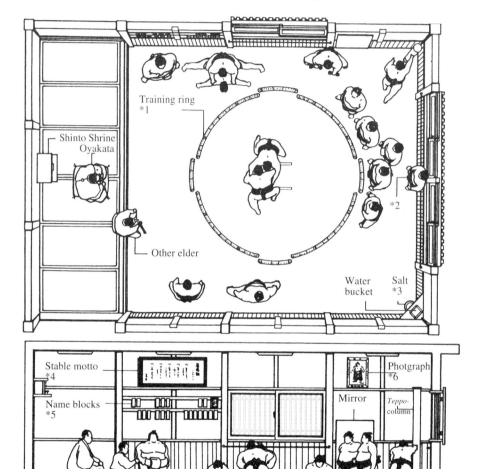

Training ring *1

Shinto Shrine
Oyakata

Other elder

*2

Water bucket

Salt *3

Stable motto *4

Name blocks *5

Photograph *6

Mirror

Teppo-column

*1. The size and shape of the training ring is exactly the same size as that used in tournaments.
*2. A rikishi who leans against the wall in the training room and tries to loaf off is called *kamaboko*.
*3. Salt is used to purify the ring, and also to rub into cuts and scrapes to prevent infection.
*4. Each stable has its own motto.
*5. Each elder, rikishi, and other employee has his own name plate. They are arranged by rank.
*6. Photos of a stable's most successful rikishi are displayed.

Haridashi Information | Rikishi use cotton mawashi for training. The training mawashi is 2mm thick, 47cm wide, and 100m long, with the length adjusted to individual rikishi.

The sumo stable is home to its rikishi. Young rikishi live and train with their stablemates as they work towards the goal of achieving *sekitori* status.

Younger rikishi have water ready for *sekitori. Sekitori* may also stand by with water for senior rikishi who have helped them along in the past. This is no more than common courtesy.

Bamboo pallet Used to scrape off sand and dripping sweat

Purifying the Ring after Practice

When practice is over, rikishi trainees clean up and purify the ring. Next they sweep a pile of sand into the center, shape it into a mound, and put a sacred staff (*gohei*) on top of it. Finally, they fling salt on the ring in three directions from the edge of the ring, and offer a prayer.

This purification ceremony is repeated each day.

Each stable has its own variations on this rite.

Shinto shrine

The mound of sand is shaped into a pentagon, angled directly in line with the Shinto shrine in the room.

gohei

gohei

salt

A Day at a Sumo Stable Schedule

A Day at a Sumo Stable

4:30 am Wake up

5:00 am Training begins
The lowest ranked rikishi are the first to begin.

7:00 am *Sekitori* wake up

8:00 - 11:00 am
Sekitori begin their practice session. The elders enter the training room and watch from the raised platform in the room.

| Haridashi Information | Rikishi are allowed to have their own rooms only after they achieve juryo status. Trainees live together in a single large room. |

The sumo stable is the foundation of the sport and its unique society. There the stablemaster lives with his rikishi and they lead a communal lifestyle. Even on the road, a stable attends to the details of daily life, taking care of its own cooking, laundry, and so on. The routine described on these pages does not apply to tournament periods.

11:30 am Bath time
top-ranked rikishi go first.

Attendants for a bathing *sekitori*

Bathe in order

12 noon Mealtime
As usual, *sekitori* go first.

Rikishi eat twice a day. Lunch is our main meal.

Trainees stand by and serve

2:00 pm Nap time

Everyone takes a nap!

Lunch is over by 1:30. Trainees have to clean up before they can rest.

4:00 pm Wake up

See you at dinner!

They also do the laundry and clean house.

I'm on chanko duty!

6:00 pm Dinner

The menu may be curry rice or other homestyle dishes.

We *sekitori* like to eat out!

10:00 pm Curfew

Free time after dinner

Most stables have a 10 o'clock curfew

11:00 pm Lights out

···· Good night

Early risers go to bed early!

A Typical Training Session

matawari (leg stretching)

To avoid injury!

Stretch out your legs and touch your torso to the ground.

moshiai (elimination-style wrestling)
The winner of a practice bout remains in the ring for another bout.

The winner gets to choose his next opponent.

suriashi (foot dragging)

The basic foot movement walking without lifting one's feet from the ring.

shiko (stamping)

A boasic move…

for strengthening legs and back.

We also train with weights and other equipment.

teppo (steel columns)

Exercise for strengthening upper body and arms, Also helps to master leg movements.

Haridashi Information

A form of practice where the loser has to remain in the ring until he beats somebody is called *makenokori*. *Kachioshi makeoshi* (win or lose) is when a wrestler fights all comers regardless of the outcome of each bout.

Rikishi build up strength and polish their techniques during their daily practice sessions. Read below to find out some of the different ways they practice in their *beya* training room.

Rikishi vie to be next.

sanbangeiko (three-bout practice)
Two rikishi wrestle several bouts together until they have had enough.

Let's go again!

butsukari-geiko (hitting)
Sides are divided into passive and active, with the active side running full force into the chest of the passive rikishi.

Attacking helps improve impact and strength, and helps rikishi learn to avoid injury.

Ow!

Ow!

Outside Practice
Most practice is done in one's own stable, but rikishi will sometimes visit other beya if their own has only a few rikishi or if someone wants to practice with a rival who they have trouble beating. Sometimes related stables will hold a joint practice session.

White-bearded Inosuke

The 19th Shikimori Inosuke

Born Takahashi Kintaro in Katsuta, Ibaragi Prefecture in 1886, this well-known character began work as a gyoji (referee) in May 1900, wan was promoted in September 1951 to the rank and name of Shikimori Inosuke. He was allowed to grow a beard because a bout of pleurisy that he suffered during World War II caused him to break out in a fever whenever he shaved his beard. Consequently, he was known in the sumo world as White-bearded Inosuke. On the first day of the September 1958 tournament, he refereed a bout between Tochinishiki and Kitanonada, the result of which was disputed and overturned by the judges. Gyoji are obliged to yield to the final decision of judges, but Inosuke was adamant and heatedly upheld his call for a full ten minutes. He did, however, relent and accepted the defeat. He was then suspended for the rest of the tournament, but it is said that he never doubted his original decision. His final tournament was in November 1959, at the age of 73. He died on December 14, 1966.

Rikishi

A Makuuchi Wrestler's Tournament Day

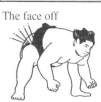
The face off

Haridashi Information During tournaments, rikishi trainees arrive at the hall earlier if they are scheduled to compete that day. Afterwards they work as attendants to makuuchi rikishi. Lower-ranked trainees with no bouts prepare meals, do laundry, and take care of other jobs at the stable.

The world of sumo is founded on ability to perform, and this is what dictates the treatment any rikishi receives. It reminds them, on a daily basis, of their success or failure, and motivates them during tournaments.

11:00 pm Lights out

10:00 pm Curfew

Gottsan desu (thanks!)

Most *sekitori* eat out during tournaments. They may treat lower-ranked rikishi to dinner or be invited out by supporters.

Afterwards, I bathe, dress, and go home.

4:10 pm Makuuchi bouts begin

Dressing Room
After entering the hall, rikishi repair to either the East or West dressing room, depending on which side they are on. Sekitori store their *akeni* (lacquered wicker trunks) in the choicest spots (in order of rank, of course), and dress in their mawashi and *kesho-mawashi* aprons.

This trainee has finished his own bout and is now attending to the *sekitori*.

akeni

Highest-ranked rikishi

TV monitor is hung from the ceiling

teppo columns

akeni

3:50 pm Makuuchi ring-entering ceremony

The Life of a Rikishi
How Rikishi Incentive Money is Computed

We jonokuchi start out with 3 yen!

Incentive money is paid only to juryo. Trainee wins and losses are computed, but they do not actually receive anything until they attain juryo status.

Trainees compete in seven bouts per tournament. If they have a winning record their basic sum will be increased.

50 sen (one-half yen) is added to the basic amount for each win of a winning record.

START

Jonokuchi
When a rikishi is listed on the banzuke, he is credited with 3 yen. 1/2 yen is added to this for each winning bout of a winning (*kachi-koshi*) tournament. A 5-win 2-loss record will add 2 1/2 yen to a rikishi's incentive.

Jonidan
Bare feet and geta

Sandanme
Sandals....

Juryo
Juryo are paid incentive money for each tournament. Juryo have their basic sums adjusted to a minimum of 40 yen upon promotion.

I finally get my incentive money!

Juryo rikishi get at least 100,000 yen per tournament in incentive money.

sekitori

A rikishi's basic incentive is never lowered for a losing record unless he is demoted from ozeki, makuuchi, or juryo ranks, in which case it is lowered to pre-promotion adjustment figures.

This loss means a demotion!

Oh dear!

Makushita
Finally gets to wear a nicer obi ↓

Makuuchi
The minimum amount for a makuuchi rikishi is adjusted to 60 yen.

This works out to 150,000 yen per tournament.

We have to win at least eight bouts to have our incentive increased.

A record of 9-6 means an increase of 1 1/2 yen

Haridashi Information | The highest basic incentive figure ever achieved by a rikishi was 1489 1/2 yen by yokozuna Taiho. This record is followed by yokozuna Chiyonofuji's 1447 1/2 yen and yokozuna Kitanoumi's 1216 yen.

When a rikishi is promoted to juryo, he receives a salary for the first time, and he also receives incentive money for each tournament. This figure is based on the career wins and losses of each wrestler and multiplied by 2,500. Therefore the 40 yen basic sum of a juryo rikishi comes to ¥100,000 per tournament.

Our basic incentive figure is multiplied by 2500. We receive it even if we do not compete in a tournament.

There is treasure buried in the ring!

Yokozuna
The basic figure for a yokozuna is adjusted to 150 yen, but most yokozuna have achieved this minimum figure before promotion.

A yokozuna will always receive at least 375,000 yen per tournament.

Makuuchi Championship
A tournament winner has 30 yen added to his basic incentive amount. A 15-0 record will gain him 50 yen.

trophy

¥75,000 yen per tournament for each championship.

Gold star
Rikishi have 10 yen added for beating a yokozuna.

Gold star!

That means ¥25,000 per tournament.

Ozeki
The minimum basic figure for ozeki is 100,000 yen.

I get at least 250,000 per tournament

...and usually more!

The Life of a Rikishi
His Possessions

Underwear
A rikishi wears a loose cotton undershirt (short sleeves in winter, sleeveless in summer), cotton boxer shorts and knee pants (*suteteko*). The undershirt is designed with a wide neck and buttons so that he can put it on and take it off without mussing his topknot.

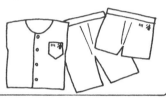

Lion-do in the Ryogoku neighborhood and other specialty shops provide us with extra-large clothes and accessories.

Our *tabi* are made at Ryogoku's Kikuya Tabi Shop

Short-sleeved undershirt

The name of the rikishi is sewn onto the breast pocket.

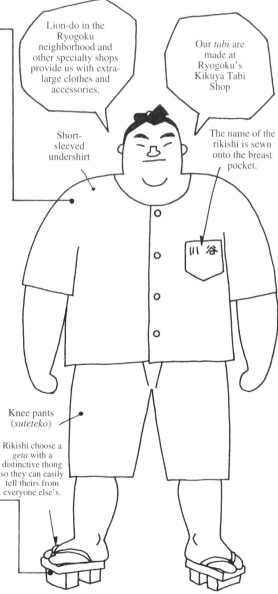

Tabi (socks)
Worn only by makushita rikishi and above. The soles are triple-reinforced. Formal tabi are made of cotton or silk and have five clasps (*kohaze*) up the back. *Tabi* for practicing are twice as thick, with reinforced stitching on the soles.

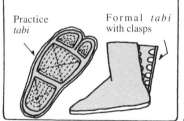

Practice *tabi*

Formal *tabi* with clasps

Knee pants (*suteteko*)

Rikishi choose a *geta* with a distinctive thong so they can easily tell theirs from everyone else's.

Geta (wooden sandals)
The *geta* worn by jonokuchi and jonidan are made of the hardest parts of the paulownia tree. The blocks on the soles are twice as thick as those on regular *geta*.

Haridashi Information | Rikishi usually buy their footwear between tournaments and tours. This is because one way to express "spend money" is "to put one's foot out." Rikishi are very superstitious and they

In sumo society, one can see many aspects of Japan that are no longer a part of mainstream society. This includes the *chonmage* topknot, *tabi*, *geta*, kimono, and so on. To make the matter of acquisition even more complicated, rikishi are so large that they can rarely buy anything off the rack. There are several shops that are instrumental in supporting the tradition of the sport by providing clothing and accessories in the sizes required by sumo wrestlers.

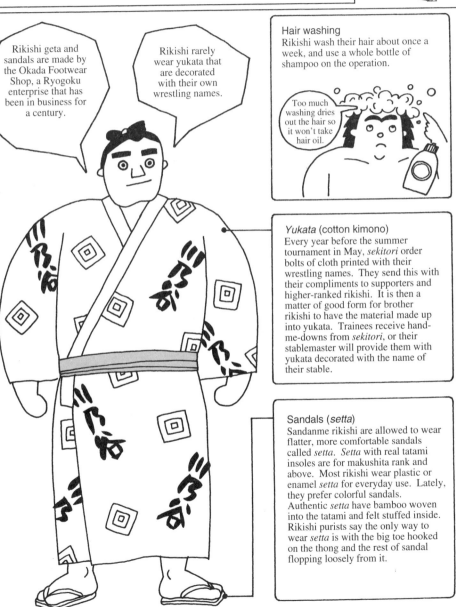

Rikishi geta and sandals are made by the Okada Footwear Shop, a Ryogoku enterprise that has been in business for a century.

Rikishi rarely wear yukata that are decorated with their own wrestling names.

Hair washing
Rikishi wash their hair about once a week, and use a whole bottle of shampoo on the operation.

Too much washing dries out the hair so it won't take hair oil.

Yukata (cotton kimono)
Every year before the summer tournament in May, *sekitori* order bolts of cloth printed with their wrestling names. They send this with their compliments to supporters and higher-ranked rikishi. It is then a matter of good form for brother rikishi to have the material made up into yukata. Trainees receive hand-me-downs from *sekitori*, or their stablemaster will provide them with yukata decorated with the name of their stable.

Sandals (*setta*)
Sandanme rikishi are allowed to wear flatter, more comfortable sandals called *setta*. *Setta* with real tatami insoles are for makushita rank and above. Most rikishi wear plastic or enamel *setta* for everyday use. Lately, they prefer colorful sandals. Authentic *setta* have bamboo woven into the tatami and felt stuffed inside. Rikishi purists say the only way to wear *setta* is with the big toe hooked on the thong and the rest of sandal flopping loosely from it.

73

do not want the purchase of footwear to lead them to put their foot out of the ring and suffer a loss.

The Life of a Rikishi II
Akeni, kesho-mawashi, and *chanko-nabe*

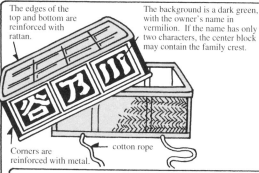

The edges of the top and bottom are reinforced with rattan.

The background is a dark green, with the owner's name in vermilion. If the name has only two characters, the center block may contain the family crest.

cotton rope

Corners are reinforced with metal.

Akeni (lacquered wicker trunk)

This is how *sekitori* carry their necessities around with them. The trunk is made of woven bamboo, covered with *washi* (Japanese paper), and finished with a cashew-based paint. Inside, a rikishi has his *kesho-mawashi*, mawashi, a change of clothing, and so on. On the first day of a tournament, one of the rikishi's attendants will carry his trunk into the dressing room at the tournament hall, and there it will remain until the final day.

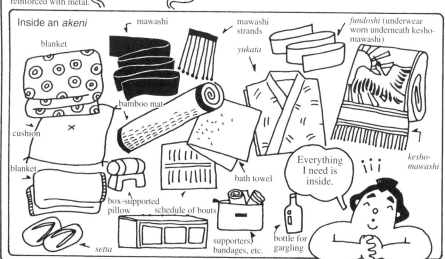

Inside an *akeni*

blanket

mawashi

mawashi strands

yukata

fundoshi (underwear worn underneath kesho-mawashi)

cushion

bamboo mat

blanket

box-supported pillow

schedule of bouts

bath towel

setta

supporters, bandages, etc.

bottle for gargling

Everything I need is inside.

kesho-mawashi

The *hakata*-weave silk cloth is embroidered with more than twenty colors of silk thread, including silver and gold. The weight of the embroidery thread alone comes to about a kilogram.

The name of the presenter is embroidered at the bottom.

Fringes. Only ozeki and yokozuna are allowed to have purple fringe.

The *Kesho-mawashi* Apron

This is the brightly-colored apron that a *sekitori* wears for ring-entering ceremonies. The cloth used is 68 cm in width and six to nine meters in length. It is folded and sewn into the proper length. The picture depicted on the front is embroidered and the fringe attached. The resulting product weighs about 10 kg. When the yokozuna makes his ring-entering ceremony, his *kesho-mawashi* and those of the herald and sword bearer are made as a matching set.

Haridashi Information | Makuuchi wrestlers have "tournament cushions" with their names sewn on. They fold it in two and sit on it next to the ring as they wait for their bout to be announced. Their attendants

When a rikishi is promoted to juryo and receives the title of *sekitori*, he can then own a wicker trunk (*akeni*) and *kesho-mawashi*. These two prize possessions, inscribed with his name, are tangible signs of a rikishi's rise through the ranks.

Chanko-nabe (One Pot Meals)

Chanko is a name that summarizes most of the one-pot meals that rikishi eat. This is what the rikishi of a stable eat when they are all together for a meal. Otherwise they tend to eat dishes served in most Japanese households. People tend to think of *chanko* as a particular dish, but it is really just a name for one-pot meals. There are a number of different types, and each stable has its own specialties. Below are recipes for two different *chanko-nabe*.

Sakana Chiri

Ingredients: codfish, sea bream, bluefish, and other fish in season. Bok choy, bean sprouts, shiitake mushrooms, enoki mushrooms, leaks, chrysanthemum leaves, spinach, and tofu.

Directions: Fill a pot with water and boil. Then add fish. Next add chopped vegetables and tofu in order of time required to cook, and simmer until tender (add tofu and chrysanthemum leaves last, boiling for no more than a few minutes). Each person takes out the ingredients they want to eat, dipping them in small, individual bowls of vinegar and soy sauce (*ponzu*) mixed with finely-grated daikon, carrot, and onion.

Serve the pot before the chrysanthemum leaves have changed color and become too mushy. By putting the pot on a hot plate on the table, fresh vegetables can be added as needed.

Soup Taki

Ingredients: chicken, daikon (giant white radish), carrots, burdock root (*gobo*), onions, eggplant, chrysanthemum leaves, spinach, fried tofu skins (*abura-age*), and konnyaku.

Directions: Make stock by boiling the chicken carcass with sugar, soy sauce, mirin (sweet sake), and sake to taste. All other ingredients, including chicken, should be chopped into bite-sized pieces. Pour the soup into a big pot and add ingredients in order of time needed to cook. Start with the chicken, then add daikon, carrots, burdock root, and so on, putting in the chrysanthemum leaves last.

Later, you can put udon noodles or rice cakes (*mochi*) into the soup. Simmer and eat

A good dish for a crowd because no dipping sauce is required.

Rikishi and "Good Luck"

Rikishi are very superstitious and they always like to have good luck on their side. This is called *gen wo katsugu* or "shouldering good fortune." Each rikishi has his own precautions and practices. After a losing bout, he may go out and change some item of his attire in an attempt to "change his luck."

A black mark indicates a loss.

red

Never use black ink before a bout for an autograph or a hand print

Never wash the good luck out of a topknot...

...or shave during a a a winning streak

...or change *kesho-mawashi*...

Take a different road to the tournament hall during a losing streak...

hand them ahead of time to a yobidashi who puts them out for rikishi as they make their entrances.

The Drummer Who Led the Resurrection of Grand Sumo
Yobidashi Taro
(1888-1971)

Born Toguchi Sadajiro in Tokyo 1888, he became a yobidashi at the age of eleven and eventually became famous as the drummer Yobidashi Taro. In 1904, led by Genjiyama, he left the then Tokyo Sumo Association. Taro then wandered throughout the country until the birth of the Japan Grand Sumo Association in 1927. After World War II, he was one of the persons instrumental in reviving sumo. He traveled around the country, calling the scattered yobidashi back to their profession. He also worked to improve the status of yobidashi. It was at his request that yobidashi were included, albeit temporarily, on the official banzuke ranking chart. In 1960, at the age of 72, he retired from his position, but continued to work in the JSA Press Club. It was to his great regret that, once again, the names of yobidashi were deleted from the banzuke. In 1969 he was decorated with the Sixth Order of Merit. He died on March 3, 1971.

Tournament

Tournament Details
From the *Gomen-iwai* to the First Day

Gomen-iwai (Tournament Announcement)

Held on an auspicious day about one month before a tournament begins. Members of the press are invited and given a schedule for the coming competition.

Tickets Go On Sale

Ticket sales usually begin three to four weeks before a tournament begins. In the case of the Nagoya tournament in July, however, tickets can be purchased as early as mid-March.

Banzuke Announcement

The newest rikishi rankings are announced on a Monday thirteen days before a tournament. This is pushed back to sixteen days for the January tournament because mailing takes longer during the New Year's season.

The *banzuke* is my New Year's card!

Happy New Year!

Raising the Scaffolding

One to two weeks before a tournament, on an auspicious day, the scaffolding (*yagura*) is raised by the JSA equipment maintenance department. This group is also in charge of posting the wooden *banzuke* and putting out the colorful banners decorated with the names of individual rikishi.

It takes eight professionals all day to put the *yagura* up.

Observation of *Keiko* by the Yokozuna Judging Committee

One week before a Tokyo tournament, the members of the Yokozuna Judging Committee are invited to the Sumo Training School in the Ryogoku Kokugikan to watch a training session which includes yokozuna, ozeki, and upper makuuchi-ranked wrestlers.

All yokozuna and ozeki come.

Haridashi Information If a wrestler decides to sit out a tournament after a bout is scheduled, his opponent wins by default. Bouts are then reworked so that there will not be two defaults in a row.

There are six regularly-scheduled tournaments a year. The Tokyo JSA Business Division handles details for tournaments in Tokyo (January, May, and November). Those held in March (Osaka), July (Nagoya), and November (Fukuoka) are left to the care of organizations in each of those cities.

New Apprentice Examination

New apprentice examinations are held five days before a tournament. Those who pass have their first official pre-sumo (*maezumo*) bouts beginning two days after the tournament opens.

Making the Ring

Four or five days ahead of time, about twenty yobidashi assemble to prepare the ring, and this takes three days. When it is completed, the roof is hung over it and the drapes and four tassels attached.

Drapes

Tassel

We yobidashi make the ring. No mechanical equipment is used.

Empty beer bottles are used to put on the finishing touches.

Tamper (*tako*)

This is also used to tamp down the dirt

Bout Compilation Conference

Two days before opening day, the judges assemble to set bouts for juryo and makuuchi rikishi for the first two days of the tournament.

Ring Celebration and Drum Beating

The day before a tournament opens, a ceremony is held to purify and pray over the ring. Afterwards the drummers enter, circle the ring three times, leave the hall and parade through the neighborhood to advertise the next day's bouts.

Day One

This is it!

The Roof and the Ring

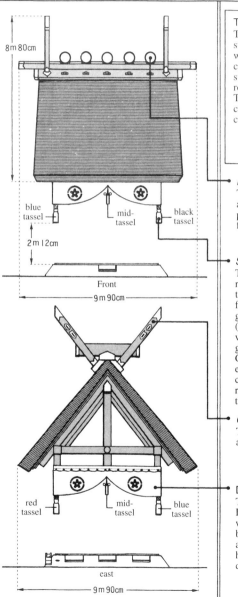

8m 80cm

blue tassel

mid-tassel

black tassel

2m 12cm

Front

9m 90cm

red tassel

mid-tassel

blue tassel

east

9m 90cm

The Roof Over the Ring (*tsuri-yane*)

The roof over the ring is constructed in the *shinmei* style usually seen on Shinto shrines. Formerly, it was built over the ring and supported by four columns. This was replaced in 1952 by a roof suspended from the ceiling by wires. The hanging roof in the Ryogoku Kokugikan weighs six tons. The framework is made of aluminum alloy and covered by the wood of *keyaki*, zelkova, and cryptomeria trees.

Katsuogi

The tubular-shaped figures on the roof ridge pole are called *katsuogi*. These are symbols used to pacify the ring. The roof in the Ryogoku hall has five of these.

Shibusa (Four tassels)

These tassels, each of a different color, are symbolic replacements for the columns that used to support the roof, and they represent the four directions, the four seasons and their four gods. Blue is east (spring) guarded by the Blue Dragon god; red is south (summer) guarded by the Vermilion Sparrow god; white is east (autumn) guarded by the White Tiger god, and black is north (winter) guarded by the Black God of Water. The tassels are made of spun embroidery thread. They are 210 cm in length, 66 cm in width, and weigh 17.8 kg each. There is a regulated distance of 212 cm between the tassel and the surface of the ring.

Chigi

The boards that stick out diagonally from the roof are called *chigi*, and they symbolize immobility.

Drapes

The drape is made of purple cloth 120 cm in width. It bears the crest of the Japan Sumo Association in white. It is first attached to the black side, then the blue, red, and white. Each side is lifted in the middle and decorated with a smaller tassel. These tassels have the same colors as their corresponding directions.

Haridashi Information	Since ancient times, the sumo ring has been considered a holy place where rikishi polish their skills and compete. Traditionally women have been forbidden to tread on it. Even today, no woman is allowed to enter the ring for any reason.

The ring is said to originate from the days of exhibition sumo held by Oda Nobunaga in 1576. During the Edo Era, tubular bales were first used to make a double-circle ring. The ring finally evolved into its present form in 1931. This section provides illustrations and diagrams to accompany explanations about the ring and hanging roof.

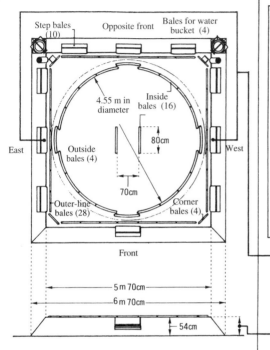

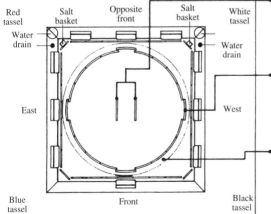

The Ring (*dohyo*)

Clay-like dirt is used to make the ring, requiring about 30 tons to do the job. Merely replacing the surface takes eight tons. To make the ring, 66 rice bales of six varieties, are used. Each variety has its own purpose, and they are stuffed with dirt, sand, and gravel. The height of the bales protruding from the dirt of the ring is stipulated in the rules of competition. About sixty-percent of a bale is buried, leaving a little less than half visible. The inside bales are about 5 cm high, with the ones protruding outside the circle (*tokudawara*) only slightly higher.

Nijiguchi

These are the entrances to the ring located in the centers of the east and west sides. The name, which means "character for two," is derived from the resemblance of the outside bale and the one used as a step to the character for "two." Rikishi enter on the east and west side.

Height of the Ring

Regulations require it to be between 54 cm and 60 cm high.

Shikiri-sen (face-off lines)

The *shikiri-sen* lines are painted in white enamel with the yobidashi doing touch-ups every day during tournaments.

Tokudawara (outside bales)

These are the bales placed slightly outside the circle of the ring at the center of each side: east, west, north, and south. These were originally used to let rainwater drain from the ring.

Janome-no-suna (bull's eye sand)

This refers to the sand that is spread on the outside of the ring to a width of 25 cm. Judges often check it during a close call to see whether or not a rikishi actually did step out of the ring, leaving a footprint. To make the job easier, yobidashi keep it neatly swept for bouts.

Basic Sumo Knowledge I
Sumo Terms for Body Parts and Mawashi Belts

Shimekomi
This is the formal mawashi belt that juryo and higher-ranked rikishi wear during competition. The belt is satin and in either one of two traditional weaves, *nishijin* or *hakata*. The belt weighs between four and six kilograms. The original fabric is 80 cm wide and is eight to twelve meters in length. It is folded in six and then wrapped around a rikishi five or six times. Rikishi will customarily break in a new belt during an exhibition tour so that it will be ready for use during a regular tournament.

A tall rikishi with long arms is referred to as "deep chested" (*futokoro ga fukai*) because of his capacity for enveloping his opponent or for keeping him away from his mawashi. This type is difficult to push out or throw down, making him a sticky opponent.

Maemitsu
This refers to the outside layer of the front of a belt. A rikishi will often grab this part of the belt of his opponent in order to pull him off balance. If the belt becomes loose, the gyoji will most likely halt the bout to retie it.

Sagari
The strands that are tucked into the belt. *Sekitori* have theirs starched. There are always an odd number of strands, with nineteen being the most common. Sumo trainees have fewer strands, and theirs are made of limp cotton.

Maetate mitsu
The vertical portion of the front of the belt. Grabbing this section or sticking fingers into it is prohibited during competition, and will result in an automatic loss for the offender.

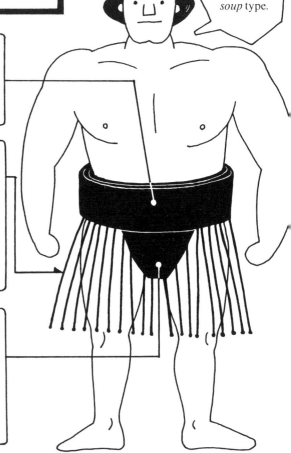

I'm a *soup* type.

Haridashi Information | A *shimekomi* is never laundered. It is wiped off with a cloth and hung out in a shady spot. Because women are never supposed to touch a belt, men handle every step of production, from order-taking to delivering the final product.

The sumo society has its own lingo. This is the same as with other industries, such as TV, newspapers, and magazines. Learning the lingo and the meanings behind the words will make watching sumo even more fun. In this section, learn the words rikishi use for equipment, body types, and so on.

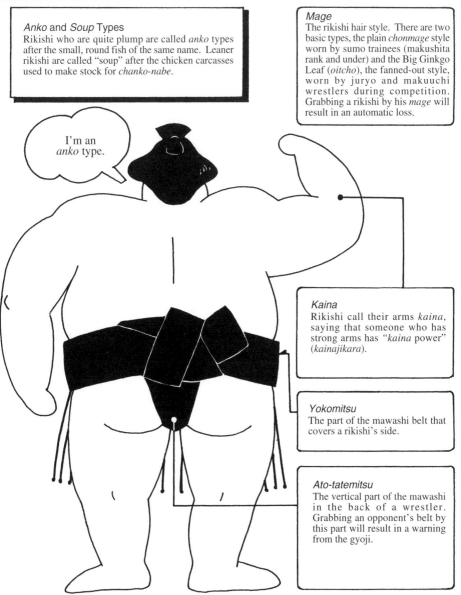

Anko and Soup Types
Rikishi who are quite plump are called *anko* types after the small, round fish of the same name. Leaner rikishi are called "soup" after the chicken carcasses used to make stock for *chanko-nabe*.

Mage
The rikishi hair style. There are two basic types, the plain *chonmage* style worn by sumo trainees (makushita rank and under) and the Big Ginkgo Leaf (*oitcho*), the fanned-out style, worn by juryo and makuuchi wrestlers during competition. Grabbing a rikishi by his *mage* will result in an automatic loss.

I'm an *anko* type.

Kaina
Rikishi call their arms *kaina*, saying that someone who has strong arms has "*kaina* power" (*kainajikara*).

Yokomitsu
The part of the mawashi belt that covers a rikishi's side.

Ato-tatemitsu
The vertical part of the mawashi in the back of a wrestler. Grabbing an opponent's belt by this part will result in a warning from the gyoji.

Sonkyo

Basic Sumo Knowledge II
Ring Manners and Ceremonies

Manners in the Ring

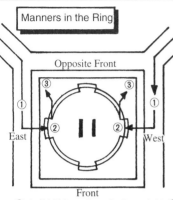

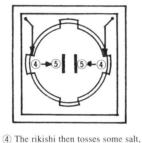

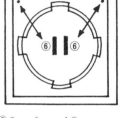

① A rikishi bows from the *hanamichi* (aisle from the dressing room to the ring), and then sits below the ring while waiting for his bout.

② The yobidashi and gyoji announce the rikishi, and he goes to the entrance of the ring, bows and steps up.

③ An east rikishi stands under the red tassel, a west rikishi under the white, stamps and then receives the "strength water" (*chikara-mizu*).

④ The rikishi then tosses some salt, goes through the *chirichozu* motions (see diagram below).

⑤ He then moves to the *shikiri-sen* lines in the center of the ring to stamp and meet his opponent.

⑥ Steps four and five are repeated several times until the time comes for the beginning of the bout. [The fight actually begins by unspoken mutual signal.] The limit for this pre-bout facing off is four minutes for makuuchi, three minutes for juryo, and two minutes for all lower ranks.

There are "strength water" buckets under both red and white tassels. After I rinse my mouth out, I use a piece of "strength paper" to wipe off my mouth and face. This is for purification.

Chirichozu is made in a crouching position. First of all, arms are lowered as shown in the illustration below ① . Then the rikishi claps his hands ②, and holds his arms out again, turning the palms up and down ③.

We fling salt to exorcise malice from the ring and purify it.

Haridashi Information When a rikishi performs a "hand sword" (*tegatana*) motion as a form of thanks, the three gods being appeased are Ame-no-Minakanushi, Takami-musubi, and Kami-musubi.

Sumo society is said to "begin and end with a bow." Indeed, many ancient customs are still observed. The beauty of sumo is supported by these traditions which have been passed on faithfully from generation to generation.

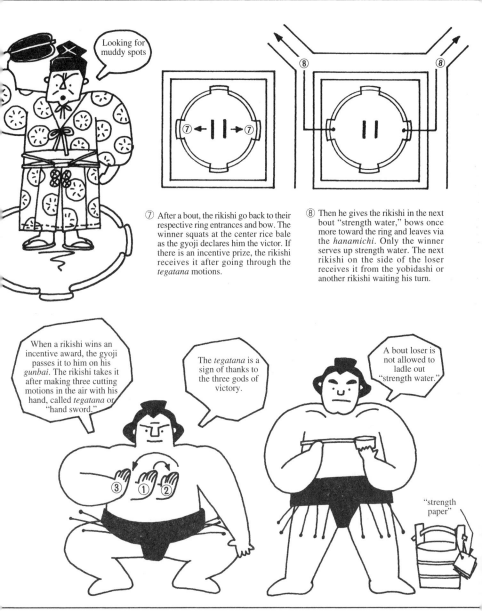

Looking for muddy spots

⑦ After a bout, the rikishi go back to their respective ring entrances and bow. The winner squats at the center rice bale as the gyoji declares him the victor. If there is an incentive prize, the rikishi receives it after going through the *tegatana* motions.

⑧ Then he gives the rikishi in the next bout "strength water," bows once more toward the ring and leaves via the *hanamichi*. Only the winner serves up strength water. The next rikishi on the side of the loser receives it from the yobidashi or another rikishi waiting his turn.

When a rikishi wins an incentive award, the gyoji passes it to him on his *gunbai*. The rikishi takes it after making three cutting motions in the air with his hand, called *tegatana* or "hand sword."

The *tegatana* is a sign of thanks to the three gods of victory.

A bout loser is not allowed to ladle out "strength water."

"strength paper"

Basic Sumo Knowledge III
Fundamental Sumo Techniques and Terms

Drums

Tachiai (Bout beginning)

Tachiai (Bout beginning)

The basic *tachiai* consists of the combatants crouching, bending, and putting their fists to the ground, all the while maintaining eye contact with each other. The instant their "breathing synchronizes" the battle begins.

Atari (Contact)

There are different moves in which the wrestlers come into contact with each other: attacking with the head, bending elbows at right angles and going for an opponent's jaw or throat, pushing one hand against the chest, and aiming for an opponent's entire body. Some bouts last no longer than a few seconds. Obviously, the first contact achieved after the *tachiai* is vital to achieving an advantageous position.

Henka (Change)

Henka is achieved by making a move that anticipates an opponent's initial attack by moving to the right or left to avoid it, reduce the amount of impact, and so on. This sort of change during a *tachiai* is often called "making an order" or "settling the bill."

Tobidogu (Jumping equipment)

Using a leg or kicking technique to achieve a victory just as the bout begins.

Nekodamashi (Cat fooling)

A surprise-attack method that entails clapping one's hands in front of an opponent's face to throw him off balance and attain an advantageous position.

Pushing

Tsuppari (Hitting)

Using the palm of one's hand to push at an opponent's face or chest. One method involves pushing alternately with each hand, another uses both hands at the same time.

Harite (Slapping)

This is the technique of slapping an opponent in the face with the palm of the hand at the onset of a bout to achieve *yotsu-zumo* (see facing page).

Hazu (a word that describes part of a bow)

A hand position in which the thumb and forefinger are spread apart. A *hazuoshi* (*hazu* push) involves putting a hand in the *hazu* position under an opponent's arms and pushing up.

Nodowa (Necklace)

Pushing at an opponent's neck with a hand in the *hazu* position (see above). Basically, one hand is in the *nodowa* position while the other fends off an *ottsuke* attack (see below).

Ottsuke (Push off)

Twisting an opponent's outstretched arm up and outside. This is a basic technique that is used for both offense and defense.

Shibori (wring)

Grabbing an opponent's outstretched hand or elbow joint and twisting it to the inside. This is to spoil an attempt to attack with an arm.

Haridashi Information If a rikishi does not touch the ring before beginning a bout, it will be called by the gyoji or a judge, and the rikishi will return to their face-off positions.

After a bout is over, the winning move is broadcast and recorded. There are, however, a large arsenal of moves used offensively and defensively that are not recorded as winning moves but which contribute to the ferocious battles in the ring.

Yotsu-zumo (grappling duel)

Uwate (upper arm) Shitate (lower arm)

Grabbing an opponent's belt from over his arms is called *uwate*. Going in under his arms and grabbing the belt is *shitate*. This is usually used to achieve *uwate* on a wrestler's stronger arm.

Migi-yotsu, Hidari-yotsu

If both wrestlers have both of their hands on each other's belts, it is called *yotsu-mi*. *Migi-yotsu* means having a hold of a wrestler's belt under his left arm with one's right hand. *Hidari-yotsu* is the opposite position. Rikishi each have their strong hands. If two opponents have the same specialty, it is called *aiyotsu*. If it is different, it is called *kenka-yotsu*. In the latter case, a fierce battle will often ensue to get the upper hand.

Migi no aiyotsu

Gappuri-yotsu (full grapple)

Both rikishi have both hands on each other's belts in advantageous positions.

Maesabaki (front rowing)

An offensive move involving dodging an opponent, pushing off his arms, and kicking him in order to achieve an advantageous position.

Morozashi (completely in)

Also called *nihon-zashi*, or "two arms in." Having both arms at an opponent's side under his arms. It is considered a good move to be able to bend one's elbows out and push. Letting an opponent achieve *morozashi* is called *sotoyotsu*.

Kannuki (door bolt)

Getting a grip on an opponent's arms which are in the *morozashi* position and twisting them upwards.

Hanmi (half body)

Stretching out one's arm, pulling one leg back, and facing to the side. This position lets a rikishi attack while in a strong position.

Nozokaseru (allowing a peek)

Not being able to get between an opponent's arms and sides deeply enough, allowing a peek of the attacking wrist from the outside.

Sashide o kaesu (returning the attacking arm)

Putting one's elbow under an opponent's arm and putting the back of one's hand on his back. By doing this, an opponent cannot get *uwate*, and the outstretched arm is neutralized. It is also called *kaina wo kaesu*.

Mawashi o kiru (cut the mawashi)

Twisting one's hands, elbows, or waist to get an opponent's hands off one's mawashi.

Makikae (rewinding)

Thrusting one's arm under the arm of one's opponent in order to get into a better position.

Gaburiyori

Making an advance by jolting one's body against an opponent while maintaining hold of his mawashi.

Winning Moves I
Basic, Throw, and Trip Techniques

Sword bearer

kihon-waza basic techniques

tsuki-dashi
thrust out

tsuki-taoshi
thrust down

oshi-dashi
frontal push-out

nage-waza throws

shitate-nage
under-arm throw

uwate-nage
over-arm throw

kote-nage
arm-lock throw

kubi-nage
head-lock throw

ippon-zeoi
over-the-shoulder throw

nicho-nage
leg-sweep throw

yagura-nage
pendulum throw

soto-gake
outer-leg trip

chon-gake
heel-brace force-down

kiri-kaeshi
knee trip

kawazu-gake
backward -lift counter-trip

nimai-geri
ankle-sweep twist-down

komata-sukui
over-thigh scoop dump

soto-komata
under-thigh scoop dump

omata
open-stance thigh-grabbing dump

Haridashi Information If a wrestler pushes his opponent to the edge of the ring but loses because his foot leaves the ring first, it is called *isami ashi* or "over-eager foot." Picking an opponent up so that both of

Winning moves are traditionally referred to as "the forty-eight sumo moves," but there are actually seventy currently recognized by the Japan Sumo Association. The names of the moves and illustrations of each are given on the next four pages.

oshi-taoshi
frontal push-down

yori-kiri
frontal force-out

yori-taoshi
frontal crush-out

abise-taoshi
backward force-down

sukui-nage
trip throw

uwate-dashi-nage
outer arm throw

shitate-dashi-nage
inner arm throw

koshi-nage
hip-lift throw

kake-nage
arm-leg combined throw

tsukami-nage
lift throw

kake-waza trips

uchi-gake Inner-leg trip

ke-kaeshi
footsweep

ketaguri
inside ankle-kick pull down

mitokoro-zeme
triple-attack force-out

watashi-komi
thigh-grabbing push-down

tsuma-dori
open-stance thigh-grabbing dump

ashi-tori
two-handed leg tip-over

suso-tori
ankle-grabbing backward-dump

suso-harai
backward footsweep

his feet clearly leave the ground is called *okuri ashi* or "sending feet," and does not result in a loss.

Winning Moves II
Backward Pulls, Twists, Special Moves, and Prohibited Moves

Tabi

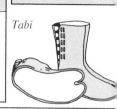

sori-waza backward pulls

izori
submarine scoop reverse-dump

tasuki-zori
shoulder sacrifice throw

shumoku-zori
bell-hammer shoulder throw

maki-otoshi
sideways twist throw

tottari
arm-bar throw

saka-tottari
arm-bar counter throw

kata-sukashi
under-shoulder swing-down

shitate-hineri
twisting under-arm throw

ami-uchi
net-casting twist-down

sabaori
forward force-down

harima-nage
rear-belt throw

hiki-otoshi
hand pull-down

hikkake
arm-grabbing force-out

hataki-komi
hand pull-down

tsuri-dashi
lift-out

utchari backward pivot throw

kime-dashi
elbow-clamp force-out

kime-taoshi
elbow-clamp force-down

yobi-modoshi
backward push-down

Haridashi Information If two rikishi fall to the ring at the same time, and the rikishi on top puts out his hands to help break his opponent's fall (*kabai-te*), it will not result in a loss for him. If the hand, however,

Besides the seventy winning moves and the two prohibited moves that decide a bout, there are eight intentional moves that are prohibited and, if used, result in a loss for the offender. These are punching with a closed fist, grabbing an opponent's hair, jabbing at the solar plexus or other vital parts, pulling both ears simultaneously, pulling at the *maetakemitsu* of the mawashi, grabbing the throat, kicking the chest or stomach, and bending back one or two fingers.

kake-zori
leg-kick sacrifice throw

sototasuki-zori
cat-fooling throw

hineri-waza
twists

tsuki-otoshi
thrust down

soto-muso
outer thigh-grabbing twist-down

uchi-muso
inner thigh-grabbing twist-down

zubu-neri
elbow-twist throw

uwate-hineri
twisting over-arm throw

kaina-hineri
two-handed arm twist-down

gassho-hineri
clasped-hands twist throw

kubi-hineri
twisting-head throw

tokushu-waza
special moves

tsuri-otoshi
lift-dump

okuri-dashi
rear push-out

okuri-taoshi
rear push-down

wari-dashi
upper-arm force-out

higi (shobu-kekka)
prohibited moves (bout decision)

isami-ashi
over-eager foot

koshi-kudake
back smasher

is made to prevent his opponent from reversing the bout result (*tsuki-te*), it will be called as a loss.

A Typical Tournament Day
The Time Schedule

Rice bales

A Typical Tournament Day

8:00 a.m. *Yose-daiko* drums

Drums on the scaffolding are beat at the start and close of the day by young yobidashi.

The first bouts begin anywhere from 9:30 to 11:50 depending on whether there is pre-sumo beforehand. Pre-sumo bouts are held on even-numbered tournament days, and followed by jonokuchi.

9:30 a.m. Jonokuchi bouts begin.

Hall lights are kept dim until later.

10:30 a.m.   Jonidan bouts
12:00 noon   Sandanme bouts
1:30 p.m.   Makushita bouts
2:40 p.m.   Juryo ring entering ceremony

2:50 p.m.   Juryo bouts
3:30 p.m.   JSA greetings

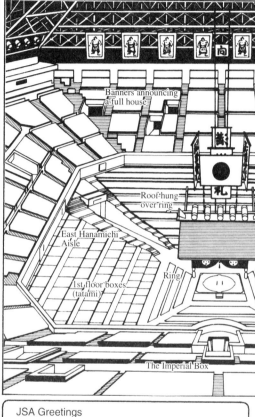

Banners announcing a full house

Roof hung over ring

East Hanamichi Aisle

Ring

1st floor boxes (tatami)

The Imperial Box

JSA Greetings
On the first and last days of a tournament, the chairman of the board of trustees comes into the ring, accompanied by the top makuuchi wrestlers, and sends the audience greetings from the entire JSA.

Haridashi Information   There is an electric signboard that displays the results of all juryo and makuuchi bouts and lists the names of wrestlers who are not participating in the tournament.

A tournament day begins with the drums of the yobidashi as a kind of public announcement system. Bouts are then begun, with the lowest-ranked rikishi going first. The completion of all bouts is declared with *hane-daiko* drums at the end of the day. Descriptions given below describe a day at a tournament held at the Ryogoku Kokugikan Hall in Tokyo.

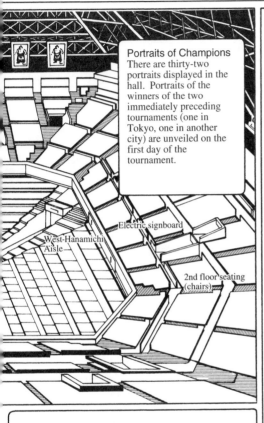

Portraits of Champions
There are thirty-two portraits displayed in the hall. Portraits of the winners of the two immediately preceding tournaments (one in Tokyo, one in another city) are unveiled on the first day of the tournament.

Electric signboard
West-Hanamichi Aisle
2nd floor seating (chairs)

3:50 p.m. *Nakairi* Intermission
The break between juryo and makuuchi bouts is called *nakairi*. During this time, the makuuchi wrestlers and yokozuna hold their ring entering ceremonies and the next day's bouts are announced. On the first day of a tournament, the championship cup and flag are officially returned during the *nakairi* break, and, at Tokyo tournaments, new portraits are unveiled.

Champion of last tournament returns flag.

Head judge

4:10 p.m. Makuuchi bouts

Bow twirling ceremony
After the final bout of the day, a makushita rikishi performs the bow twirling ceremony in praise of the winner of the final match.

A *kesho-mawashi* apron decorated with the JSA crest

The bow twirling ceremony is performed by a makushita rikishi in the same "clan" as a current yokozuna.

6:00 p.m. Bow twirling ceremony
6:05 p.m. *Uchidashi* End-of-the-Day Ceremony
The end of the tournament day is called *uchidashi* or "drumming begins."

Gyoji and Shinpan
(referees and judges)
How Bouts are Decided

If a judge questions a gyoji's call, he raises his hand and asks for a *mono-ii* (literally, "something to say") conference.

Mono-ii!

Judge on the "gyoji side" under the red tassel (timekeeper)

A gyoji's most important job is calling the tournament bouts. Even if he believes that the outcome is a tie, he must call a win for one side or the other.

Judge on the "gyoji side" under the white tassel.

East-side judge

The head judge uses a wireless microphone to announce the results of the *mono-ii* conference.

I will explain our decision. The gyoji held up his *gunbai* for the east side, but there was some feeling that there was a tie, and we have decided to call a rematch.

There will be a rematch!

Head set for communicating with the video room.

Head judge on the "front" side

Haridashi Information

Phrases used to announce the results of a *mono-ii* include *gunbai doori* or "just as the gyoji called," *dotai tori-naoshi* "tie and rematch," and *gunbai sashi-chigai* "gyoji reversal." *Mono-ii* can also be called in order to confirm a hand or foot touching the ring.

The results of bouts are entrusted to the gyoji in the ring and the five judges sitting around it. Judges take full responsibility for all outcomes and call for a *mono-ii* conference when they have a question about the gyoji's decision. These two pages describe how a *mono-ii* is called and what it entails.

When a *mono-ii* is called, all five judges climb into the ring. The head judge asks each member for his opinion and then they discuss it.

The gyoji can give his opinion but he does not vote on the final outcome.

Bout judging
Bout decisions are made by the Judging Committee who divide themselves into groups of five. This committee is also in charge of time keeping and recording statistics.

West-side judge

A ring-side rikishi may also call a *mono-ii*.

The Video Room
The JSA has used videotape replays as an aid to resolve bout outcomes since May 1969. The elder in the video room will replay a bout only at the request of the head judge. He then describes the bout as he sees it but does not vote on the final decision.

The head judge uses a head set to contact the video room and get a description of the bout as replayed. This is then considered when making the final decision.

I listen to the elder in the video room.

How do you see it there?

Head judge

I don't give an opinion, I just tell the others what I see.

Elder in the video room (Judging Committee member)

Rikishi A's foot leaves the ring just as Rikishi B falls.

Joy and Sorrow in the Ring

Kachi-koshi!!

Kachi-koshi (a winning record) and *make-koshi* (a losing record)

For juryo rikishi and above, who compete in fifteen bouts per tournament, *kachi-koshi* is eight wins. For makushita and under, who have seven bouts, it is four victories. Anything lower is *make-koshi*, a losing record. All *kachi-koshi* rikishi can look forward to a pay raise and a promotion. *Make-koshi*, just as surely, means a demotion. A rikishi trying for his eighth win of a tournament refers to the bout as "pay-day sumo." If he wins it, he calls it "revised salary."

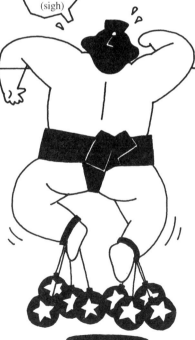

...make-koshi... (sigh)

ooh...

Occupational Injury

When a rikishi is hurt in the ring, it is called an occupational injury and he is allowed to stay out of one tournament and still maintain his *banzuke* rank. All five judges who observed the bout must verify the injury to make it official. If the claim is submitted within three days after the fact, the decision can be discussed and settled between two members of the Occupational Injury Committee and Judging Committee.

I can only sit out one tournament. Injuries incurred out of the ring are not classified as occupational injuries.

| Haridashi Information | The opposite of "reformed salary" (see above) is "the other side of pay day." When a rikishi achieves his first win of a tournament it is called "putting out the first day" or "opening the eyes." |

On the last day of a tournament, after fifteen days of well-fought bouts, some rikishi go back to their stables with winning records and smiles on their faces. Others return with the desire to improve their record in the next tournament. This section describes promotions, demotions, injuries, and tournament prizes — events that can fill a rikishi's heart with joy or sorrow.

Sansho

Sansho are the three prizes for which makuuchi rikishi are eligible other than the championship. The Outstanding Performance Prize (*shukun-sho*) goes to the rikishi who wins the most bouts with ozeki and yokozuna. The Fighting Spirit Prize (*kanto-sho*) is awarded for a spectacular performance that builds up the excitement during the tournament. The Technique Prize (*gino-sho*) is given to the rikishi who is able to demonstrate his mastery of difficult techniques. These three prizes were first awarded as a part of the November 1947 tournament. Yokozuna, ozeki, and rikishi with losing records are not eligible for the *sansho*, and no award is made if it is determined that there are no suitable candidates. The decision is made by the Sansho Judging Committee. The committee meets on the final day of a tournament to determine the winners who then receive a certificate, trophy, and one million yen each in prize money.

The Outstanding Performance Prize goes to the rikishi who beats the most yokozuna and ozeki.

The Fighting Spirit Prize rewards a brilliant tournament performance.

The technician

The Technique Prize is for the rikishi who best demonstrates excellent sumo technique.

The Champions

After the juryo bouts are completed on the final day of a tournament, the awards ceremony is held for the champions of jonokuchi, jonidan, sandanme, makushita, and juryo ranks, with each receiving a certificate and prize money. If there are ties for any of the ranks, playoff bouts are held before the ceremony.

If three or more rikishi tie for a championship, round-robin bouts are held until one rikishi wins two bouts in a row.

Jonokuchi   Jonidan   Sandanme   Makushita   Juryo

The Makuuchi Championship I
From the Final Bout to the Victory Parade

Slapping

The Schedule for *Senshuraku* (the final day of a tournament)

10:50 a.m. Jonokuchi bouts
11:30 a.m. Jonidan bouts
12:50 p.m. Sandanme bouts
 2:00 p.m. Makushita bouts
 2:15 p.m. Juryo Ring Entering Ceremony
 2:35 p.m. Juryo bouts
 3:10 p.m. JSA Greetings (see p.92)
 3:15 p.m. Awards Ceremony
Play-off bouts are held if there are ties for championship titles
 3:25 p.m. *Nakairi* Intermission
Makuuchi Ring Entering Ceremony
Yokozuna Ring Entering Ceremony
 3:45 p.m. Makuuchi bouts
 5:15 p.m. *San'yaku* Assembly

The final three bouts on *senshuraku* are called *yaku* sumo, and the winners receive, in order, a bow, a bowstring, and an arrow. If there is a runoff for the championship, the playoff bout is held about ten minutes after the final bout.

 5:45 p.m. Makuuchi Awards
The champion is presented with the Emperor's Cup and many other prizes.
 6:10 p.m. Sansho Awards Ceremony (see previous page)
 6:20 p.m. Presentation Ceremony for New Apprentice Rikishi

Deciding Bout

I win!

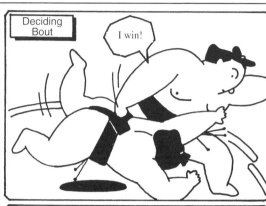

The Photograph

The champion moves his wicker case to the most prestigious spot in the east dressing room and is photographed with the Emperor's Cup.

The Victory Parade

Traditionally, the champion rides from the Kokugikan to his stable in a convertible with the top down, waving to well-wishers along the way.

A rikishi from the same clan carries the Championship Flag.

Haridashi Information	If there is a three-way tie for first place, a round-robin playoff is held. Rikishi draw straws to determine the contenders of the first bout. The winner then plays the remaining rikishi, and so on until one of the three wins two bouts in a row.

All makuuchi rikishi compete for the greatest honor in sumo, the Makuuchi Championship, the final outcome of fifteen days of tournament competition. This section gives a typical schedule of activities during the final day (*senshuraku*) of a regular tournament, including a description of the awards ceremony and victory parade.

Interview With the Champ

After the deciding bout, the new champion is interviewed in the dressing room..

I get interviewed while my barber fixes my topknot.

The Emperor's Cup

A championship trophy was first awarded after the January 1926 tournament. The Emperor's Cup in current use was first presented to the winner of the January 1928 tournament. The names of winners are engraved on silver name plates attached to the base of the cup.

When all of the name plates have been engraved, they are set into a plaque and a new set attached to the cup.

There are eighty name plates attached to the base

Awards Ceremony

The JSA Chairman presents the Emperor's Cup, and the head of the Judging Committee gives the Championship Flag.

Back at my Stable, we'll hold a championship party.

The Championship Flag

The Championship Flag was first introduced in 1909. At the time, the competition was between east and west, with the flag going to the side with the most makuuchi victories. The current practice of presenting the flag to individual winners began in 1947.

The flag used now is the fourth one. It was made in 1991 at a cost of 9.5 million yen.

The flag is passed on to the next champion, but winners get to keep a certificate.

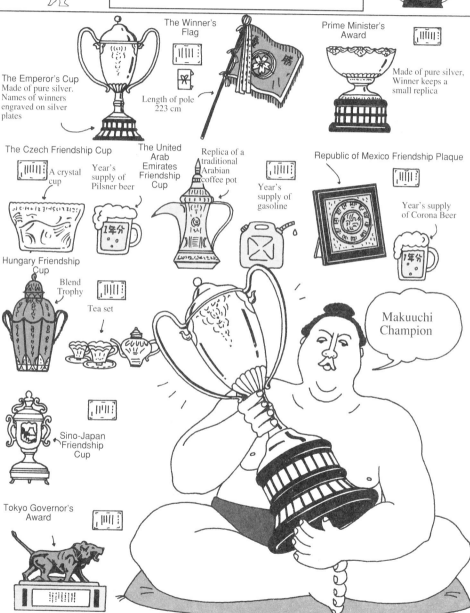

The Winner's Flag

Length of pole 223 cm

Prime Minister's Award

Made of pure silver, Winner keeps a small replica

The Emperor's Cup
Made of pure silver. Names of winners engraved on silver plates

The Czech Friendship Cup

A crystal cup

Year's supply of Pilsner beer

The United Arab Emirates Friendship Cup

Replica of a traditional Arabian coffee pot

Year's supply of gasoline

Republic of Mexico Friendship Plaque

Year's supply of Corona Beer

Hungary Friendship Cup

Blend Trophy

Tea set

Makuuchi Champion

Sino-Japan Friendship Cup

Tokyo Governor's Award

Haridashi Information | The photograph of the champion displayed in Kokugikan is a black and white photograph highlighted with oil colors. It is unveiled on the first day of the next Tokyo tournament.

The rikishi who battles his way to the makuuchi championship is showered with awards and prizes from all over the world. Those illustrated on these two pages are presented to the champion of a tournament at the Ryogoku Kokugikan inTokyo.

Winner's Photograph
(Mainichi Shimbun Newspaper)

The size of six tatami mats!

(Winner keeps a miniature replica)

The NHK Cup

Tokyo Shimbun-
Tokyo Chunichi
Sports Award

Japan Agriculture Asso. Prize

30 bales of rice
10,000 hot-spring eggs

Oita Shiitake Agricultural
Cooperative Award

Cup full of shiitake mushrooms

Oita dried mushrooms

Fukui Prefecture Governor's Award

Trophy

One ton of Fukui dried plums

Hokuren Award

One four-ton truck full of Hokkaido butter and asparagus

Miyazaki Governor's Award

One whole Miyazaki beef cow (ready to eat)

Aiichi Produce Cooperative Award

1500 bottles of Aiichi orange juice

Trophy

Shizuoka Agriculture, Forestry, and Fishery Association Award

Champion's weight in Shizuoka green tea

Matsue Mayor's Award

One ton of Yamato clams

Clean Campaign Award

10,000 bars of soap

JAL Award

The JAL Trophy

Sake-no-Tsukasa Ozeki Award

Filled with top-class sake

Four barrels of Ozeki sake

Coca Cola Award

Bon Merci Award

High-class Swiss wrist watch

Isuzu Motors Award

One Isuzu Big Horn

(Awarded at the May 1992 Summer Tournament)

certificate

prize money

101

Preparing for a Tour

Preparing for a Tour

Let's have sumo in our town!

A written application is made to the JSA.

Application

The JSA Tour Division

The JSA holds tours four times a year after regular tournaments. The locations that have requested the tour pay contract money to the Tour Division and the location receives permission to sponsor sumo. Sponsors are allowed to keep all remaining proceeds from the event.

The elder in charge of the Tour Division visits the site to make sure all of the conditions have been met and to explain proper procedures. If everything is in order, the application is accepted.

Necessary Conditions for Holding a Sumo Tour Event

Capital
15 million yen is required. This includes 5.5 million yen paid to the Tour Division, hall rental, accommodations and so on.

Hall (gymnasiums, etc.)

300 to 350 rikishi go on tour. Providing a bath for us is another condition.

Hotel accommodations

OK!

I make the final check

Contract
A tour is scheduled, and a contract signed three months beforehand. 20% of the contract money is paid at this time with the rest to be paid on the day of the event.

Here's the schedule!

Schedule

Sponsor

Tickets are on sale!

The majority of profits are made on tickets.

20% of the fee (1.1 million yen)

Tour Schedule
The main touring areas are the same from year to year. The Kinki and Chugoku regions in April, Tohoku and Hokkaido in August, the Tokai region in October, and Kyushu in December.

Haridashi Information Although all ranks of rikishi participate in the tour, there are some who stay at home. They are called *nokori-ban*, or "on duty at home."

All tours are handled by the JSA Touring Division. One purpose of tours is to give fans in outlying areas a chance to see sumo up close, and another is to drum up support for the sport. This section will give you an idea of how a tour is organized.

Elders not in the Tour Division are in charge.

Wakaimonogashira take care of housekeeping.

We make sure preparations are underway.

Ten days before a scheduled event, one elder goes to the different locations to take care of preparation.

Arranging accommodations

Inspecting the hall

Everything looks fine

Rikishi are assigned to hotels commiserate with their rank.

Making the ring

In order to avoid waste, a ready-made base is covered with a plastic sheet onto which dirt is packed.

Arranging transportation — trains, buses, taxis, etc.

We yobidashi take care of the final touches.

The right kind of dirt must be found for the ring.

The base is a collapsible wooden one packed with plastic beer cases.

Train timetable

The rikishi entourage arrives the day before a scheduled event. When the JSA truck pulls up, the lower-ranking rikishi begin unloading luggage and cooking utensils which they take into the dressing rooms.

After the truck is unloaded, we do laundry and run errands.

Cooking Tools

大相撲○○場所

Japan Sumo Association

The cooking pot weighs 70 kg

What Happens on Tour

A Touring Day Schedule

Lower-ranked rikishi arrive at the hall before day breaks. They make meal preparations and then begin their training session.

7:00 am	Training for lower-ranked wrestlers begins *During the next two hours *sekitori* begin to arrive and practice outdoors. Wrestlers in charge of cooking get to work.
9:00 am	Juryo training begins
10:00 am	Makuuchi training begins
11:00 am	Bouts begin (either jonokuchi or jonidan bouts) Sandanme bouts begin *After they work out, the rikishi bathe and then eat, highest ranks first. The makushita and lower-ranked wrestlers wait on the *sekitori* while they wait for their bouts to be announced.
11:30 am	Makushita bouts begin *taiko* drumming
12:55 am	*Shokkiri* (comic performance)
1:30 pm	Sumo *jinku* (folk songs)
1:45 pm	Juryo ring-entering ceremony
1:50 pm	Juryo bouts begin
2:00 pm	*Nakairi* (break before makuuchi bouts begin)
2:10 pm	Hair-dressing demonstration
2:20 pm	Demonstration of how the ceremonial rope is tied to the yokozuna
2:30 pm	Makuuchi ring-entering ceremony Yokozuna ring-entering ceremony
2:40 pm	Greetings by sponsor
2:50 pm	Makuuchi bouts begin Bow-twirling ceremony
3:15 pm	Finish

After the day's program is completed, the entourage cleans up and travels onto the next stop on their schedule.

Shokkiri

Two lower-ranked wrestlers perform some moves that are very unusual or that are forbidden during regular bouts. This is a comic interlude for the audience.

One wrestler is thin and the other large and heavy. At times even the gyogi gets in the action.

Kicking the stomach is forbidden

Whaddaya think yer doing!

Sumo *jinku*

Lower-ranked wrestlers come into the ring and sing the form of folk song unique to the world of sumo. The performance usually includes tunes about the district they are touring through.

Hai! Dosuk dosukoi!

Haridashi Information After the bouts are over, the lower-ranked wrestlers load the trucks and the entire group heads for the next location. During tours rikishi usually travel by bus or on chartered trains.

When sumo comes to town the fans are in for various attractions never shown during regular tournaments, and have a chance to interact with their favorite rikishi. This section offers a sampling of sumo activities during a touring event.

Taiko Drumming

> Sponsors may ask to have rikishi from the same stable compete against each other.

> Actual bouts are not as fierce as tournament battles, just enough to make an appearance

> Demonstration of the various drums used on tournament days.

Wakaimonogashira make sure the program runs smoothly.

> .... We will also demonstrate sumo hair dressing

Yobidashi act as MCs. →

Touring and Training

Wrestlers are most interested in tours as a chance to get in some extra training sessions. Lower ranks begin to warm up before sunrise, followed in order by rikishi of higher ranks. Even *sekitori* make their appearance by 7 a.m. Rikishi waiting for their chance in the ring begin their work outside, drawing a circle in the dirt for their boudaries. Makuuchi rikishi begin training indoors at about 10 a.m. Everyone works out for about an hour.

> This is a good time to study techniques of other rikishi.

Overseas Performances

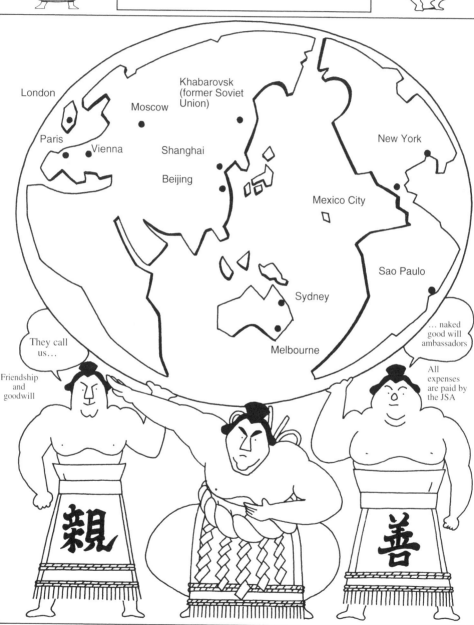

London

Khabarovsk
(former Soviet
Union)

Moscow

Paris

Vienna

Shanghai

New York

Beijing

Mexico City

Sao Paulo

Sydney

Melbourne

They call
us…

Friendship
and
goodwill

…naked
good will
ambassadors

All
expenses
are paid by
the JSA

Haridashi
Information

Overseas performances follow the same schedule of ring-entering ceremonies and bouts as in regular tournaments.

The JSA made its first overseas performance in 1965 with a trip to Moscow and Khabarovsk. (in present-day Russia). Since that time (and as of April 1998), the JSA has visited many different cities in nine countries. The purpose of going overseas is to introduce sumo to other cultures and act as goodwill ambassadors for Japan. No matter where they go, sumo performances are received with excitement and enthusiasm. Read on for highlights of sumo performances overseas.

Moscow and Khabarovsk

July 25 to August 10, 1965
The JSA ventures overseas for the first time at the invitation of the Ministry of Culture of the former U.S.S.R. Under the leadership of the elder Dewanoumi, forty-eight rikishi including four yokozuna demonstrated their sport in the cities of Moscow and Khabarovsk.

Mexico City

June 1-6, 1981
To promote goodwill and mutual understanding between Japan and Mexico. Yokozuna Kitanoumi and 111 other rikishi went to Mexico City, lead by the elder Kasugano (ex-yokozuna Tochinishiki), where they offered three days of sumo to an enthusiastic audience.

Paris

October 7-16, 1986
The sumo debut in Europe took place in Paris. All makuuchi rikishi made the trip, with yokozuna Chiyonofuji as the main attraction. The three-day exhibition was attended by standing-room-only crowds.

London

October 5-15, 1991
A Japan Festival was held to commemorate the one hundredth anniversary of the Japan-Great Britain Society, and the JSA was invited to take part in events with five days of exhibition sumo. An entourage of 106 rikishi, including yokozuna Kitashoumi played to packed houses.

Beijing and Shanghai

April 3-17, 1973
Sumo was performed to commemorate the normalizing of relations between Japan and China. The elder Musokawa led 116 rikishi, including two yokozuna to Beijing and Shanghai where they performed for a total of six days.

New York City

June 10-19, 1985
All makuuchi rikishi, including two yokozuna, participated at the three-day tournament-style event in New York's Madison Square Garden.

San Paulo

June 4-15, 1990
A three-day sumo performance was held in Sao Paulo in order to promote goodwill and cultural exchange between Brazil and Japan. Ninety-eight rikishi participated under the leadership of the elder Futagoyama (the former yokozuna) Wakanohana.

Vienna and Pari

October, 1995

Melbourne and Sydney

June, 1997

There were also tours to Spain and Germany in 1992, and to the U.S. (San Jose, California and Hawaii) in 1993.

Making a Ring Overseas

The rings for overseas performances are made by the yobidashi and other JSA staff that precede the main entourage. Dirt with a high clay content is located and collected, and bales brought from Japan are embedded in it. The hanging roof (tsuri-yane) is the one used at regular tournaments outside of Tokyo. In this way, it is possible to introduce sumo to overseas fans in an authentic manner.

Television Broadcasts I
Live NHK Sumo Broadcasts

The broadcast car

A live sumo broadcast requires twelve TV cameras, all of which send their displays to the broadcast car. There the program director decides which will be broadcast on TV, switching from one view to the next.

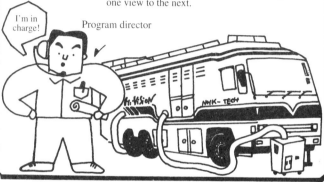

I'm in charge!

Program director

Broadcasting from the Ryogoku Kokugikan Hall

Bird's eye view is shot from the back of the third floor

2nd and 3rd floor seats

Front

The broadcast station at the front side (*shomen*) of the arena.

The announcer and one blow-by-blow reporter sit in the broadcast seat on the front side of the ring. The announcer acts as the MC, pulling together and mixing commentary from the reporter next to him. Another is on the opposite side of the hall and the *hanamichi* reporter speaks with the rikishi as they come out of the dressing room and make their way to the ring.

The floor director. She relays messages back and forth from the program director to the announcer.

My monitor shows the same picture viewers see on TV.

The TV monitor

I act as the overall MC, using the picture on the monitor as a guide. I only watch the ring about a quarter of the time.

The reporter

Receiver

Receiver stays in his ear during the entire broadcast

NHK broadcasts begin at about 3:10 p.m., English broadcasting on NHK BS at about 4:30.

Haridashi Information	The NHK sumo broadcast with the highest rate of viewership ever was the final day of the July 1993 tournament when yokozuna Akebono, and brothers ozeki Takanohana, and

NHK began live sumo broadcasting in 1953. After color transmissions began in 1965, rikishi began wearing more colorful mawashi.Below is a brief description of how broadcasts are handled and who is involved in them.

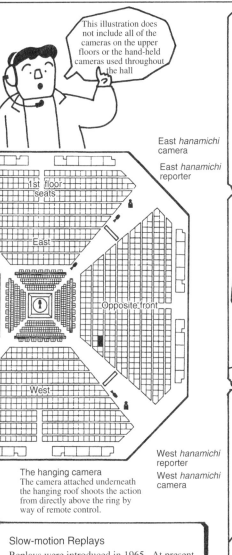

This illustration does not include all of the cameras on the upper floors or the hand-held cameras used throughout the hall

East *hanamichi* camera

East *hanamichi* reporter

1st floor seats

East

Opposite front

West

West *hanamichi* reporter

West *hanamichi* camera

The hanging camera
The camera attached underneath the hanging roof shoots the action from directly above the ring by way of remote control.

Slow-motion Replays
Replays were introduced in 1965. At present, it is possible to replay the immediately preceding bout from four different angles.

The Interview Room
The hall is equipped with an Interview Room where rikishi who have won a particularly important or exciting bout are interviewed for TV.

Announcer

That was a great bout!

Whew

puff puff

The "opposite front side" (*muko-shomen*) announcer's seat
There is usually one reporter in this spot, supplementing the main announcing from a position closer to the action.

Elder doing the reporting

Floor director

The winning move was *uwate*.

Receiver

TV monitor

Hanamichi reporter
One announcer is stationed at both the East and West *hanamichi*.
They report on the expressions on the faces of the rikishi who have just completed their bouts and occasionally get a comment. Keeping an eye on events in the dressing room is also part of this reporter's job.

I have 15 to 20 seconds to get a few words from rikishi.

sekiwake Wakanohana held a three-way play off for the championship. Akebono beat his opponents before they had a chance to fight each other.

Television Broadcasts II
Behind the Nightly "Sumo Digest"

The Announcer's Day

9:00 a.m.: Wake up

I spend about two hours planning.

· · · · ·

With a show to produce each night, I don't spend much time on morning training sessions during tournaments.

12 noon to 2:00 p.m.: Enter the tournament hall

I check in at the Sumo Press Club for any updates.

I greet the *oyakata* who is that evening's guest.

Reporting
The announcer follows the bouts, taking notes for use during the program.

I sit in the reporter's section in Tokyo and the press seats at other tournaments.

I practice my delivery.

Takes about an hour.

Confirm the bouts for the next day and write notes on cards kept on individual rikishi.

Haridashi Information One reason that NHK is the only network that carries tournaments live is because of its nationwide access. Another major consideration, however, is that even if viewership declines, the public broadcasting system is the least likely to discontinue coverage.

The Grand Sumo Digest is broadcast nightly on the Asahi Network during tournaments . Viewers enjoy the reporting and statistics included in the program.

A Famous Participant in the Awards Ceremony
David M. Johns

Born in 1914 in the Philippines. After a career as a journalist in the United States, Johns came to Japan in 1958 as the Manager of Publicity in the Far East for Pan American Airways. For thirty years, beginning with the May 1961 tournament, he presented the champion with the Pan Am Award. The awards ceremony is often a dry event, but Johns never failed to draw the attention of the fans as he climbed into the ring wearing a traditional Japanese outfit complete with family crest, and read off the certificate in his own distinct Japanese. Johns loved sumo and went as far as turning down a vice-presidency position with Pan Am in order to remain in Japan. He presented his final award at the May 1992 tournament when declining health forced his retirement. This was also the last time Pan Am gave out its award, turning the trophy over to the JSA.

The Supporters of Sumo

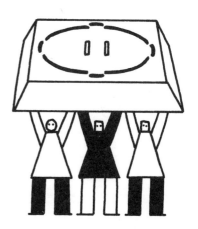

Gyoji
(Referees)

Ring Blessing

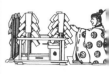

The *tate-gyoji* always presides over the final bout of the day.

The senior *tate-gyoji* goes by the name Kimura Shonosuke

Tate-gyoji always use the names Kimura Shonosuke and Shikimori Iinosuke

San'yaku gyoji get to wear tatami sandals

Tate-gyoji

Beginning a gyoji career

There are a total of 45 JSA gyoji.
Aspiring gyoji apply for the job through a stablemaster. Qualified applicants must be young men who are under the age of 19 who have completed compulsory education. They must have good eyesight, perfect hearing, and a sound body.

San'yaku

I learn how to make calls using the distinct gyoji pronunciation, pausing in the proper places

The first step of an extensive training period!

After a gyoji is hired, he enters the gyoji stable in the Kokugikan hall and learns sumo history, how to use his *gunbai* (fan), to write in the distinct style used for the *banzuke* ranking chart, to make calls in the proper voice, and so on.

I have to learn "sumo" writing

JonidanTate-gyoji

Jonokuchi

Haridashi Information
Except in cases of demotion, gyoji are promoted in strict order of date of employment. Promotions are voted on by the board of trustees after every November tournament and go into effect from January of the following year.

The gyoji are the supporting actors of sumo. They decide the winners of each bout, decipher the winning moves, and act as masters of ceremony. They are subject to the same strict pecking order that rikishi endure, with eight different ranks to work through: *tate-gyoji* are at the top, preceded by *san'yaku*, makuuchi, juryo and four lower levels. This section will take you through the long career of a gyoji, beginning with the jonokuchi beginner.

Gyoji retire at age 65. Seniority is the basis of promotion, taking about fifteen years to achieve juryo status. Too many decision reversals is grounds for demotion (twelve for makushita and under, six for juryo and over), but a rank can be reattained the following year if a good record is maintained.

Gyoji retire at age 65

Only two ranks left to go....

I finally get to wear tabi socks!

Gyoji who reach juryo status are considered fully trained and are treated much better than colleagues at the makushita level and lower.

Bare feet

Bag boy

Last one in line

Makuuchi

I'll keep practicing my voice and my writing until they are perfect.

Juryo

Makushita

Sandanme

Kimura is "shade"

Shikimori is "sun"

"sun" is fingers facing up

The Kimuras and the Shikimoris
There are only two last names among all gyoji – Kimura and Shikimori. The two "families" each used to have their own distinct styles, but since the end of the Meiji era, gyoji change their name from Kimura to Shikimori and back again as they ascend the ranks of their profession. The only difference you will find nowadays is the way each holds the *gunbai* when they call the names of the rikishi. The Kimuras hold it with fingers facing down. Shikimoris have fingers facing up.

"shade" is fingers down

Gyoji Clothes and Accessories

Gyoji Clothes and Accessories

Tate-gyoji Kimura Shonosuke

Hakkeyoi!!

Eboshi

Hitatare

The color of *gunbai* tassels vary with rank. Shonosuke is purple.

Gunbai

Rosette

Color varies with rank. Shonosuke is purple.

Dagger

Only a *tate-gyoji* can carry a dagger. It symbolizes his resolve to kill himself to take responsibility for a problem in the ring if the need should arise.

Makushita rank and lower

The rosettes of makushita ranks and under are blue or black

Rosette

Tabi socks and tatami sandals
Gyoji of san'yaku rank and higher can wear both tabi and sandals. Makuuchi and juryo gyoji can only wear tabi

Blue or black tassels

Lower ranks wear outfits made of cotton all year round.

Bare feet

Haridashi Information When a rikishi of a particular clan is promoted to ozeki or yokozuna, the clan presents its gyoji with a new set of clothes and accessories.

As explained on the previous page, there are eight gyoji ranks, with *tate-gyoji* the highest. Gyoji wear different clothes of varying colors and carry different accessories depending on their rank. By recognizing these differences it is possible to ascertain a gyoji's rank.

Clothing

The *eboshi* hat and *hitatare* robe illustrated on the opposite page were originally worn by samurai during the Kamakura era. They came into use for gyoji beginning in 1910. Until that time gyoji wore a kimono with hakama trousers. Clothing worn in warm-weather months is made of silk gauze and gossamer. During colder times of the year, they wear heavier silk twills. Makushita and lower-ranked gyoji wear costumes made of cotton all year round. As you can see in the illustration, rosettes are sewn onto the robe of the gyoji, the colors of which are different for each rank. The JSA provides a clothing allowance for gyoji for each tournament. This is saved up and new costumes purchased. More often, however, gyoji will receive outfits from supporters or hand-me-downs from colleagues ahead of them on the ranking scale.

Gunbai

The origins of the *gunbai* date back to the Sengoku period, the Era of Warring States (1482-1558). The fan-like object was held by the shogun in order to lead his forces in battle. The *gunbai* held by present-day gyoji are made of lacquered hard woods, such as zelkova, oak, and mulberry. Some gyoji have the *gunbai* decorated with their family crest, a picture, or a motto. Each *gunbai* weighs from 750 to 1100 grams. A gyoji will use two or three different ones during a tournament, and take one with him on tour. Gyoji receive new *gunbai* from supporters, but they will often use special ones that have been passed on from one gyoji to another.

Differences Indicate Rank

It is easy to tell a gyoji's rank by the color of his rosettes, *gunbai* tassels, and footwear.

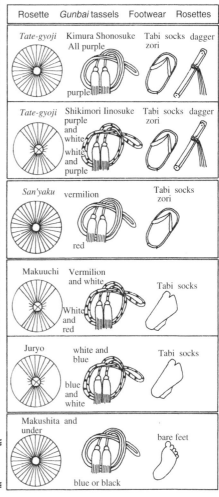

Rosette	Gunbai tassels	Footwear	Rosettes
Tate-gyoji	Kimura Shonosuke All purple / purple	Tabi socks zori	dagger
Tate-gyoji	Shikimori Iinosuke purple and white / white and purple	Tabi socks zori	dagger
San'yaku	vermilion / red	Tabi socks zori	
Makuuchi	Vermilion and white / White and red	Tabi socks	
Juryo	white and blue / blue and white	Tabi socks	
Makushita and under	blue or black	bare feet	

Heavier than you may think!

117

The Duties of a Gyoji I

Neck shove

Introductions

On odd numbered days the east side rikishi will be announced first. The west side goes first on even-numbered days.

On this side is......

The final bout of the day is between rikishi A and rikishi B....

Kimura Shonosuke referees the final bout

On this side is.......

The judge under the red tassel holds a stopwatch and lets the gyoji and yobidashi know when pre-bout time is up.

Timekeeper (judge under the red tassel)

We announce the final juryo bout and makuuchi bouts using terms of greater respect!

The gyoji for the next bout waits here

Shikiri (the face off)

The gyoji makes sure the rikishi are prepared for the face off and then get the bout underway.

No starting until both rikishi put their fists to the ground.

I call out *kamaete!* (Get ready!) during pre-bout face-off time.

When pre-bout time is up, I say *katta nashi* (no more waiting), *te-o-tsuite!* (Put your hands to the ground!)

At the moment the bout begins, I can stop and then restart the bout if the rikishi have failed to synchronize their start or if one commits an error.

118 | **Haridashi Information** | If a gyoji holds up his *gunbai* in the direction of one rikishi and then reverses his decision by moving it over to the other side of the ring, and this reversal stands as the correct decision, it is not entered onto his JSA record as a miscall.

The role of the gyoji in the world of sumo is far-reaching and can vary depending on the day. Of all of his duties, refereeing tournament bouts is his most important. Read on to find out what the gyoji is responsible for in the ring.

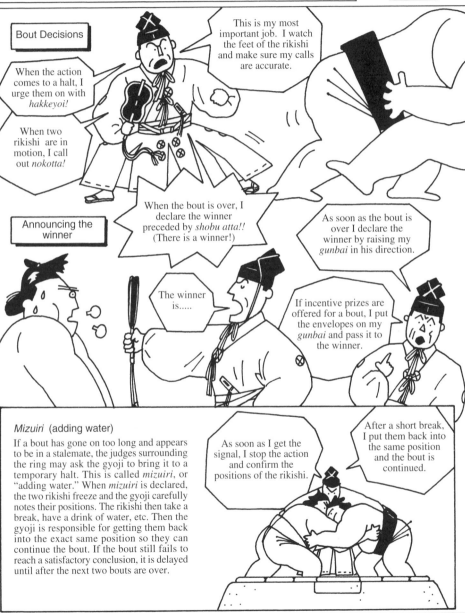

Bout Decisions

When the action comes to a halt, I urge them on with *hakkeyoi!*

When two rikishi are in motion, I call out *nokotta!*

This is my most important job. I watch the feet of the rikishi and make sure my calls are accurate.

Announcing the winner

When the bout is over, I declare the winner preceded by *shobu atta!!* (There is a winner!)

As soon as the bout is over I declare the winner by raising my *gunbai* in his direction.

The winner is.....

If incentive prizes are offered for a bout, I put the envelopes on my *gunbai* and pass it to the winner.

Mizuiri (adding water)

If a bout has gone on too long and appears to be in a stalemate, the judges surrounding the ring may ask the gyoji to bring it to a temporary halt. This is called *mizuiri*, or "adding water." When *mizuiri* is declared, the two rikishi freeze and the gyoji carefully notes their positions. The rikishi then take a break, have a drink of water, etc. Then the gyoji is responsible for getting them back into the exact same position so they can continue the bout. If the bout still fails to reach a satisfactory conclusion, it is delayed until after the next two bouts are over.

As soon as I get the signal, I stop the action and confirm the positions of the rikishi.

After a short break, I put them back into the same position and the bout is continued.

The Duties of a Gyoji II

Scissors

Announcements
The gyoji is in charge of announcing the next day's makuuchi bouts during the *nakairi* break

I will now announce tomorrow's bout combinations

yobidashi

These written combinations are called *kaobure*

Writing up the ranking chart and bout combinations
The gyoji are the only ones trained to write in the distinctive "sumo writing."

No time left!

Presiding Over Ring Dedication
The day before a tournament begins, the gyoji preside over a Shinto ceremony to dedicate the new ring and pray for safety during bouts.

This is a job for *tate-gyoji*, with Kimura and Shikimori taking turns

Tour Liaison
A gyoji accompanies the elder who goes ahead of the group during tours
His job is arranging transportation, keeping accounts, and so on.

I'd like to make reservations.

I assist the elder in charge of my stable.

Haridashi Information — During the dedication ceremony, six items are buried in the ring in order to pacify it and exorcise malicious spirits: torreya nuts, chestnuts, kelp, dried cuttlefish, rice, and salt.

Most people know that gyoji wear ceremonial robes and decide the bouts, but they also have a variety of other roles. This section gives a brief description of some of their less well-known responsibilities.

Gyoji announce the results of bouts and *kensho* prizes.

> The winning move was *yorikiri*.

> We gyoji have lots of jobs other than deciding bouts.

Recording Results
Gyoji record and confirm the results of all bouts.

> I write down bout results in the *maki*.

Preparation for bout assignments
The head of the judging committee instructs gyoji to get ready.

Work for the stable and clan
Gyoji are in charge of most of the paper work.

> Some of us keep in shape to keep up with action in the ring.

> We send out the *banzuke*.

> Sometimes we MC wedding receptions.

> ...let's welcome the bride and groom.

The Yobidashi

There is a maximum 45 yobidashi in the JSA, and the retirement age is 65. Yobidashi are JSA employees, but each is attached to a particular stable. After a young man is employed, his colleagues teach him how to make the distinctive yobidashi calls and use the wooden clappers.

Yobidashi Attire

This is the fro-o-n-t of a yo-o-bi-i-dashi!

I wear a kimono and knee-pant style *hakama*.

White silk fan

Japan Sumo Association

The Yobidashi Union

The official structure includes a yobidashi union that is attached to the JSA, but we actually work for individual stables

The JSA pays our salaries

These leggings are called *tattsuke-bakama*. They are loose down to the knees and then wrap around the lower legs like gaiters. They are supplied to yobidashi by corporations or other sponsors.

Tabi with rubber soles

Haridashi Information

The "purifying salt" used in the ring is either raw salt or refined salt that has been mixed with water to make it rough in texture. An average of 40 kilograms a day is used during tournaments, for a total of about 600 kilograms for the entire fifteen days.

Chic in their *tattsuke-bakama*, yobidashi stand in the ring, spread out their white fans, and call out the names of the rikishi in the next bout. The yobidashi does not have a particularly flashy job, but it is vital to the workings of sumo. Employees of the JSA, yobidashi each have home stables where they take care of various routine duties. Read this section to learn about the outward appearance of the invaluable yobidashi.

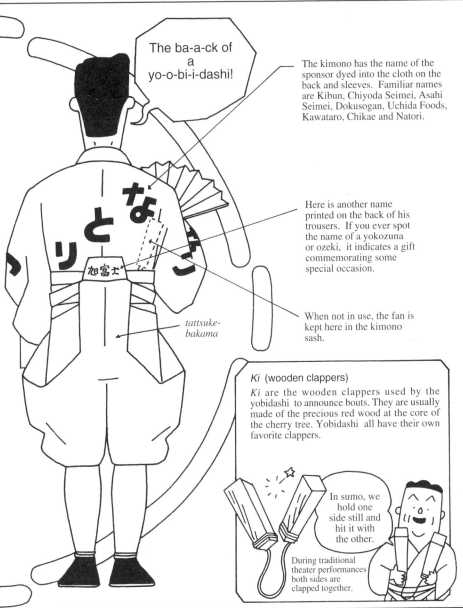

The ba-a-ck of a yo-o-bi-i-dashi!

The kimono has the name of the sponsor dyed into the cloth on the back and sleeves. Familiar names are Kibun, Chiyoda Seimei, Asahi Seimei, Dokusogan, Uchida Foods, Kawataro, Chikae and Natori.

Here is another name printed on the back of his trousers. If you ever spot the name of a yokozuna or ozeki, it indicates a gift commemorating some special occasion.

When not in use, the fan is kept here in the kimono sash.

tattsuke-bakama

Ki (wooden clappers)

Ki are the wooden clappers used by the yobidashi to announce bouts. They are usually made of the precious red wood at the core of the cherry tree. Yobidashi all have their own favorite clappers.

In sumo, we hold one side still and hit it with the other.

During traditional theater performances both sides are clapped together.

The Work of Yobidashi

Hazu push

Fure-daiko
The day before a tournament begins, the yobidashi circle the neighborhood, announcing the bouts for the next day.

Sumo begins tomorrow! Come see some exciting bouts!!

We do the announcing while on tour and help sell souvenirs, too.

Yobi-age
The most glamorous duty of a yobidashi. He enters the ring, spreads his fan and announces the rikishi in the next bout.

I'm in peak condition today!

On the e-e-a-st si-i-i-de is Sasani-i-i-shi-ki, Sasani-i-i-shi-ki,!

We also take care of housekeeping at our stable.

Cleaning the Ring
We use a broom to get rid of any stray objects around the ring, making sure it is clean and pure. Before a bout we sweep all around the outside of the rice bales.

Water
We take care of the strength water, paper, and towels used by the rikishi. We also let them know when pre-bout time is up.

When a rikishi takes a fall, we grab the water bucket to prevent injuries. We have to stay on our toes!

We also run the book and souvenir stalls inside the Kokugikan Hall.

Making the Ring
Before every official tournament, twenty yobidashi spend three days making the ring. They also go from stable to stable making and maintaining stable practice rings, as well as preparing the rings for all tour events.

| Haridashi Information | The yobidashi always use empty Asahi.beer bottles to put the finishing touches on the ring. This is because they have the shape that is easiest to grasp. |

A yobidashi is considered to have finished his training if he can make the ring announcements, use the wooden clappers properly, prepare the ring, and play the *taiko* drums. Besides these, there are other types of work that the yobidashi is in charge of. Find out what they are below.

Ki (wooden clappers)
Used to announce the next item on the day's program and as a signal. The signals are the "first warning" (it's almost time), "second warning" (get ready), and "third warning" (please enter the ring).

The scaffolding for the outside drums is 16 meters tall and the compartment at the top is 1.8 square meters in size.

The *yagura taiko* (drums on the scaffolding)
The yobidashi beat drums, or *taiko*, outside on a special scaffolding as a way of announcing a tournament. The first performance is early in the morning to bring in spectators, and the second is after the day's bouts are over. This final drumming also serves as an invitation for the crowd to come again the next day. There is no drumming after the final day of a tournament.

Kensho Banners
When a *kensho*, or incentive prize, is offered for a bout, the yobidashi carry a banner around the ring to advertise the sponsor.

...We layout cushions for ringside rikishi.

We keep the baskets full of salt.

kensho banner

We yobidashi are also in charge of keeping the face-off lines freshly drawn and touching up the ring as needed.

After the ring is completed, we string up the hanging roof, and attach the tassels and drapes.

125

Hitatare Robe

The Barber

The Barber

Up to 50 barbers are employed by the JSA. Barbers spend their first three years as apprentices. After completing that training period they are assigned to a stable. As with gyoji and yobidashi, barbers are promoted based on seniority and a five-rank system. Retirement age is 65.

First class: 18 years or more experience
Second class: 10 years or more experience
Third class: 5 years or more experience
Fourth class: Less than five years experience
Fifth class : Less than five years experience

It takes about ten years to perfect the Big Gingko Leaf. First and second class barbers can do it.

A real pro can create a Big Gingko Leaf hairstyle in 15 to 20 minutes. Each rikishi has a certain way he likes his hair done. We make sure we know all their preferences.

A barber has to have strong teeth to pull the string to tie up hair.

The only drawback is that I can never take a long vacation

Our names always include the first kanji in the word "barber."

I only spend a couple of hours a day doing topknots. After that I'm free!

Maybe I'll go get a haircut...

chonmage
This simple topknot is the hairstyle worn by makushita-rank and lower rikishi. It is also the style worn by *sekitori* on non-tournament days.

I'm dying to get a Big Gingko Leaf!

This topknot prevents head injuries, too.

See this bald spot? We shave off a small circle to make it easier to tie up a topknot. When a wrestler is close to retirement he will start letting it grow back in.

If a stable does not have its own barber, or if it has a large number of *sekitori*, it will use the services of a clan barber.

Haridashi
Information
The smell of rikishi hair is usually referred to as the "scent of *bintsuke* oil." The smell, however, is actually *suki* pomade. *Bintsuke* oil is used to soak hair in.

Barbers are employed by the JSA, but, in fact, work for individual stables. They are experts in the field of rikishi hair. Persons not connected with sumo society rarely get a look at what the sumo barbers do. Read on for an inside peek at this unusual profession.

A Barber's Equipment

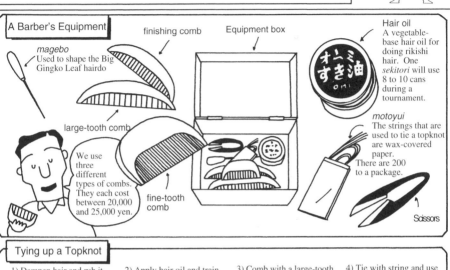

finishing comb

Equipment box

Hair oil
A vegetable-base hair oil for doing rikishi hair. One *sekitori* will use 8 to 10 cans during a tournament.

magebo
Used to shape the Big Gingko Leaf hairdo

large-tooth comb

We use three different types of combs. They each cost between 20,000 and 25,000 yen.

fine-tooth comb

motoyui
The strings that are used to tie a topknot are wax-covered paper. There are 200 to a package.

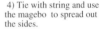
Scissors

Tying up a Topknot

1) Dampen hair and rub it to work out tangles and kinks and help the sides spread out neatly.

This makes the sides smooth.

towel

2) Apply hair oil and train with a fine-tooth comb.

Use the *mage-bo* to spread out the sides

3) Comb with a large-tooth comb and finish with the fine-tooth comb.

4) Tie with string and use the magebo to spread out the sides.

a temporary tie

Finish sides with the *mage-bo*

5) Tie up the top of the topknot and fold it over the *magebo*.

tie here

6) Tie the fold in the hair down with string and trim the end of the topknot with scissors.

tie the fold firmly

trim the end

7) Spread out the ends of the topknot and use hand and *magebo* to make sure it is even and in the proper shape.

It is the shape of the topknot end that gives this hairstyle the name *oitcho*, or Big Gingko Leaf.

All done!

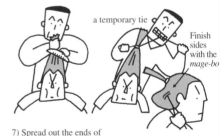
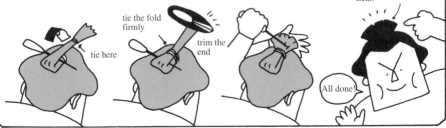

Data on Grand Sumo

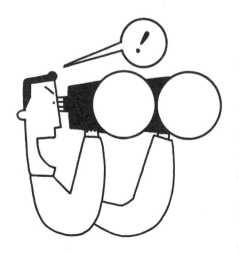

The Grand Sumo Calendar

January

- First-of-the-year training (usually January 2)
- Training observation by the Yokozuna Judging Committee (at the Kokugikan Sumo Training School)
- Yokozuna Ring-entering Ceremony at Meiji Shrine (Tokyo)
- New-apprentice Examination (Kokugikan Clinic)
- Nomino-sukune Shrine Festival (Tokyo)
- January Tournament (First Tournament) (Ryogoku Kokugikan, for fifteen days beginning on the first or second Sunday of the month.)
- Meeting of the Yokozuna Judging Committee (the day after tournament ends)
- Meeting to draw up ranking chart for the March (Spring) Tournament (about three days after end of tournament)
- Graduation and entrance ceremonies at the Sumo Training School

February

- NHK Benefit Grand Sumo (at Kokugikan, sponsored by the NHK Welfare and Culture Foundation)
- Regular Check-up (Kokugikan Clinic)
- Japan Grand Sumo Tournament (at Kokugikan, sponsored by Fuji TV)
- Yasukuni Shrine Dedicatory Sumo (Tokyo)
- Announcement of March (Spring) Tournament ranking chart (thirteen days before tournament begins
- Rikishi meeting

March

- New-apprentice Examination (Osaka Police Clinic)
- Pre-tournament festival (Sankei Hall in Osaka, sponsored by Sankei Newspaper)
- March (Spring Tournament (Osaka Municipal Gymnasium, for fifteen days starting on the second Sunday)
- Meeting of the Yokozuna Judging Committee (the day after tournament ends)
- Meeting to draw up ranking chart for the May (Summer) Tournament (about three days after end of tournament)
- Ise Shrine Dedicatory Sumo (Ise City, Mie Prefecture)

April

- Spring tour (through the Kinki, Shikoku, Chugoku, and Kanto areas, for about twenty days)
- Yasukuni Shrine Dedicatory Sumo (Tokyo)
- Announcement of May (Summer) Tournament ranking chart (thirteen days before tournament begins
- Height and weight measurements for *sekitori*, Ryogoku Kokugikan Clinic)

May

- Rikishi Meeting
- Training observation by the Yokozuna Judging Committee (Kokugikan Sumo Training School)
- New-apprentice Examination (Kokugikan Clinic)
- Yasukuni Shrine Festival (Tokyo)
- May (Summer) Tournament (Ryogoku Kokugikan, for fifteen days beginning on the second Sunday of the month.)
- Meeting of the Yokozuna Judging Committee (the day after tournament ends)
- Meeting to draw up ranking chart for the next tournament (about three days after end of tournament)
- Graduation and entrance ceremonies at the Sumo Training School

June

- Grand Sumo Elimination Competition (Kokugikan for two days, sponsored by Nihon TV)
- Announcement of July (Nagoya) Tournament ranking chart (thirteen days before tournament begins)
- Rikishi Meeting

Haridashi Information Touring, retirement sumo, and benefit sumo are referred to collectively as *hanazumo*, and a number of attractions are featured as part of the program.

During the Edo Era, someone wrote of sumo wrestlers, "lucky men who live a year off of twenty days' work." That was a long time ago. Present-day rikishi have six regularly-scheduled tournaments, six benefit tournaments, a touring schedule, and so on. Read below to find out how these busy men make their living in the late twentieth century.

July

- Atsuta Shrine Yokozuna Ring Entering Ceremony (Nagoya)
- New-apprentice examination (Chunichi Hospital)
- Pre-tournament festival (CBC Hall, Nagoya, sponsored by the Chunichi Newspaper)
- July (Nagoya) Tournament (Aiichi Prefectural Gymnasium, for fifteen days starting on the second Sunday)
- Meeting of the Yokozuna Judging Committee (the day after tournament ends)
- Meeting to draw up ranking chart for the next tournament (about three days after end of tournament)
- Summer tour: Sendai Tournament

August

- Summer tour: Sapporo Tournament (held throughout the Tohoku and Hokkaido areas from the end of July to the end of August; about 30 days)
- Announcement of September (Autumn) Tournament ranking chart (thirteen days before tournament begins
- Rikishi Meeting
- Height and weight measurements for *sekitori*, Ryogoku Kokugikan Clinic)

September

- Training observation by the Yokozuna Judging Committee (at the Kokugikan Sumo Training School)
- Yokozuna Ring-entering Ceremony at Meiji Shrine (Tokyo)
- New-apprentice Examination (Kokugikan Clinic)
- Nomino-sukune Shrine Festival (Tokyo)
- September (Autumn) Tournament (Ryogoku Kokugikan, for fifteen days beginning on the second Sunday of the month.)
- Meeting of the Yokozuna Judging Committee (the day after tournament ends)
- Meeting to draw up ranking chart for the next tournament (about three days after end of tournament)
- Graduation and entrance ceremonies at the Sumo Training School
All-Japan Rikishi Competition (Meiji Jingu Shrine, Tokyo)
- Dedicatory Sumo (Kokugikan, sponsored by TV Asahi Welfare and Culture Foundation)

October

- Autumn Tour (Kanto, Hokuriku, and Tokai areas, about fifteen days)
- King of Sumo Competition (Nagoya City Gymnasium, sponsored by Chunichi newspaper)
- Announcement of November (Kyushu) Tournament (thirteen days before beginning of tournament)
- Rikishi Meeting

November

- New-apprentice examination (Hagimoto Clinic, Fukuoka City)
- Pre-tournament festival (Fukuoka International Center, sponsored by NHK Fukuoka Broadcast Center)
- November (Kyushu) Tournament (Fukuoka International Center Hall, for fifteen days starting on the second Sunday)
- Meeting of the Yokozuna Judging Committee (the day after tournament ends)
- Meeting to draw up ranking chart for the next tournament (about three days after end of tournament)

December

- Winter Tour (Kyushu area, about twenty days)
- Announcement of ranking chart for January (First) Tournament (about sixteen days before tournament)
- Height and weight measurements for *sekitori*, Ryogoku Kokugikan Clinic)
- Rikishi Meeting

131

How to Get Seats for Sumo Events

maki

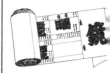

Buying Tickets

Reserved-seat tickets for a tournament go on sale on a Saturday three to four weeks before it begins. Tickets for the Nagoya Tournament in July are the exception to the rule, with sales beginning in mid-March.

Tokyo Tournaments (at the Ryogoku Kokugikan)

For January, May and September tournaments, there a total of 3720 box seats with cushions (*masu-seki*), and 11,000 seats with chairs per day. Starting with the May 1993 tournament, Ticket Pia was authorized to sell box seats, meaning that reservations can now be made by telephone. One person may reserve four box seats a day and twelve chair seats. On the first day of ticket sales reservations can be made by telephone only. Other agencies selling chair seats are the Kokugikan Ticket Office and Play Guide, with sales beginning at 9:00 a.m.
There are 500 non-reserved seats available for each tournament day. These are sold at the Kokugikan Ticket Office from 9:00 a.m. on the day they are to be used. See page 138 for types of seats and prices.

Hato Touring Buses may offer tour packages that include tournament admission. Other packages are often available through domestic airlines and the JR Railway Company.

March Tournament (Osaka Municipal Gymnasium)

Tickets for the March Tournament go on sale at the Osaka City Gymnasium on a Saturday in early February. Beginning in 1993, all reservations are made by telephone, from 9:00 a.m. to 5 p.m. every day until all tickets are sold out.

Non-reserved chair seats and standing-room-only spots go on sale each tournament morning at 9 a.m. for tickets to be used on that day. For Osaka ticket prices, see p.140.

July Tournament (Aiichi Prefectural Gymnasium in Nagoya)

Tickets for the July Tournament in Nagoya can be purchased as early as mid-March. As of publication, reservations were switched to a telephone system. As with other tournaments, unreserved tickets are sold at the gym on the day they are to be used. For more ticket information, see p.142.

November Tournament (Fukuoka International Center in Kyushu)

Tickets for the Kyushu Tournament go on sale on a Saturday in early October, and are available from The Fukuoka International Center, Iwataya Play Guide, Ticket Pia Kyushu, Tamaya (Fukuoka and Saga), Maingu Hakata Shopping Center Play Guide, Izutsuya (Ogura and Kurume), and Japan Travel Bureau (Kagoshima, Kumamoto, Oita, Nagasaki, Miyazaki, and Sasebo) agencies.

As with all other tournaments, non-reserved tickets are sold each morning at 9:00 a.m. See p.144 for more information.

Where to Buy a *Banzuke* Ranking Chart

The latest *banzuke* is usually made public on the Monday thirteen days before the next tournament begins (The January *banzuke* is announced sixteen days ahead of time). As soon as it is announced, the ranking chart can usually be purchased from the JSA Office in the Kokugikan for 50 yen. A limited number are printed, however, and they will often sell out.

| Haridashi Information | The JSA has decided to increase the number of available tickets as of May 1993, with further increases in the foreseeable future. |

Sumo fans will want to know where and when to buy tournament tickets, how to get ahold of *banzuke* ranking charts, and how support groups are organized. Read below for all the details. (It should be noted that all data is current as of July 1993).

The Sumo Annai-jo

If you enter the Kokugikan from the left-hand entrance at the front of the building, you will find yourself in a hallway lined with twenty sumo *annai-jo*, usually referred to as *cha-ya* – tea shops. These are small companies which are each commissioned to sell a certain number of tickets for each Tokyo tournament. Their official, collective name is the Kokugikan Services Company, and, as the name indicates, these *cha-ya* do more than sell tickets, they also provide refreshments to customers and act as their ushers. There are sixteen *cha-ya* in Osaka and eight in Nagoya, with each city operating under its own organization.

Buying Tickets from the *annai-jo*

The *cha-ya* have control of about seventy percent of all tickets available. Because these operations reserve almost all of their tickets for their long-time clients, other people cannot buy them. Not only are the tickets unavailable, they are largely unaffordable, with the cost of food, souvenirs, and service automatically added to the price of all tickets sold through *cha-ya*.

Dekata

The ushers who work for the *cha-ya* are referred to as *dekata*, "the person who comes out." They wear *tattsuke-bakama* outfits similar to that of the yobidashi (see p.124) and have the job of showing customers to their seats and bringing them refreshments and souvenirs. (At the Kokugikan there is also a system where customers are given a plastic card to exchange at a certain booth for a bagful of souvenirs.) It is customary to tip the *dekata* about 2000 yen, and this his main source of income. He will never ask for a tip, but if he does not receive it he will certainly register his displeasure in the quality of service he provides.

Support Groups (*koen-kai*)

At present, almost all sumo stables have support groups that provide spiritual and material assistance. Each support group has its own system of operation, but they are often based on support of a particular rikishi. Members of support groups receive ranking charts, calendars, and other souvenirs, and they are invited to observe training sessions and attend special celebrations. Some stables publish their own newsletters which they distribute to support groups, providing as much communication with them as possible, If you are interested in joining a support group for a particular stable or rikishi, contact the stable directly for further information. (See stable addresses at back of book)

The JCB Grand Sumo Club Card

The JCB credit card company, in conjunction with the JSA, now offers the JCB Grand Sumo Club Card. This is a special credit card that offers the usual credit services, but also provides users with sumo newsletters, ranking charts, calendars, rikishi hand prints, tournament ticket lotteries, and so on. Club membership fees are 7,875 yen annually. Current JCB card holders are also eligible for admission into the Grand Sumo Club. For more information, contact the JCB office nearest you.

Tokyo 03-3295-1700
Osaka 06-941-7900
Fukuoka 092-712-4450
Push-phone dial #8900 (throughout Japan)

The Ryogoku Kokugikan Hall

Mizuoke

The Kokugikan Hall

Address: 1-3-28 Yokoami, Sumida-ku, Tokyo 130-0015
Telephone: 03-3623-5111

The Ryogoku Kokugikan is located immediately to the north of the JR Ryogoku Station on a lot 18,280 square meters in size. There is a basement and three floors above ground with a total area of 38,000 square meters. Seating capacity is 11,098. On the second floor is the Imperial Box for the royal family and at the rear of the first floor is a special box for spectators with handicaps. The hall can be converted to other uses by raising the hanging roof up to the very top of the ceiling and lowering the ring and first seven rows of spectator seats into a storage area. The hall also houses the Sumo Museum, Sumo Clinic, and Sumo Training School.

Seat Prices

masu-seki A (cushions) 11,300 yen
masu-seki B (cushions) 10,300 yen
masu-seki C (cushions)   9,000 yen
A seats   8,200 yen
B seats   6,200 yen
C seats   3,200 yen
Unreserved seats.....Adults 2,100 yen,
                     Children 200 yen

How to Get to the Kokugikan on Central Tokyo Train Lines
A one-minute walk from the Ryogoku Station on the Sobu Line.

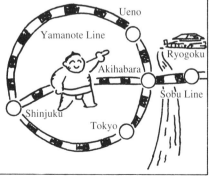

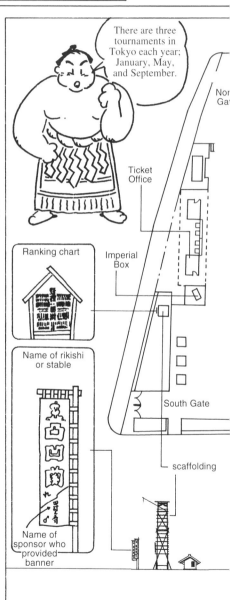

There are three tournaments in Tokyo each year; January, May, and September.

Nor Ga

Ticket Office

Ranking chart

Imperial Box

Name of rikishi or stable

South Gate

scaffolding

Name of sponsor who provided banner

Haridashi Information

The rikishi banners are made of cotton and are 90 cm in width and 5 m 40 cm long. Sponsors provide the banners. They have the name of the rikishi or stable dyed onto the cloth and then give them as gifts. Each costs about 20,600 yen and is displayed for one

The Ryogoku Kokugikan was built in 1984 as a replacement for the Kuramae Kokugikan which was built in 1954. The total cost of the new building was 15 billion yen. The first tournament held there was in January 1985.

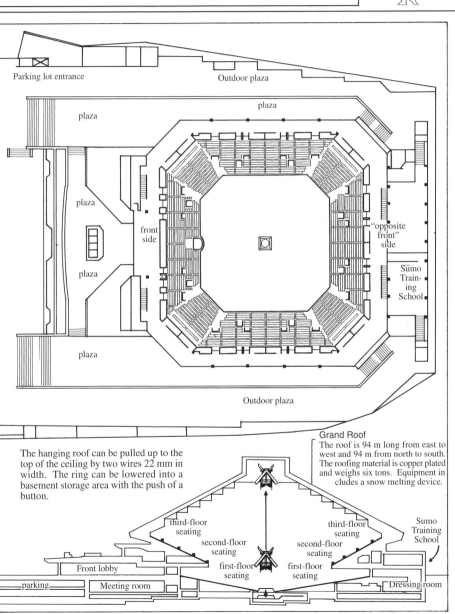

Parking lot entrance

Outdoor plaza

plaza

plaza

plaza

plaza

plaza

front side

"opposite front" side

Sūmo Train- ing School

plaza

Outdoor plaza

Grand Roof
The roof is 94 m long from east to west and 94 m from north to south. The roofing material is copper plated and weighs six tons. Equipment in cludes a snow melting device.

The hanging roof can be pulled up to the top of the ceiling by two wires 22 mm in width. The ring can be lowered into a basement storage area with the push of a button.

third-floor seating

second-floor seating

first-floor seating

third-floor seating

second-floor seating

first-floor seating

Sumo Training School

Front lobby

parking

Meeting room

Dressing room

official tournament only. After the tournament is over, JSA keeps them to use during tours and other events.

First-floor Seating at the Ryogoku Kokugikan

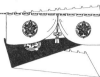

Mizuhiki-maku

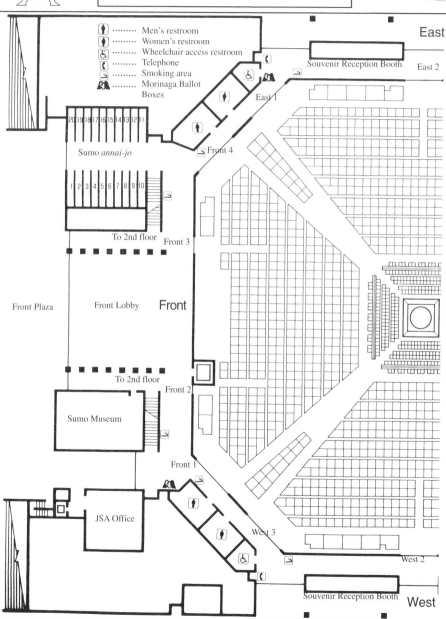

- 👨 ········ Men's restroom
- 👩 ········ Women's restroom
- ♿ ········ Wheelchair access restroom
- ☎ ········ Telephone
- 🚬 ········ Smoking area
- 🗳 ········ Morinaga Ballot Boxes

East

Souvenir Reception Booth

East 2

East 1

Sumo *annai-jo*

20 19 18 17 16 15 14 13 12 11

1 2 3 4 5 6 7 8 9 10

Front 4

To 2nd floor

Front 3

Front Plaza

Front Lobby

Front

To 2nd floor

Front 2

Sumo Museum

Front 1

JSA Office

West 3

West 2

Souvenir Reception Booth

West

| Haridashi Information | Any spectators who purchases a box of Morinaga Caramels and writes the name of his or her favorite bout of the day along with his or her name and address on the empty box, is eligible |

The *tamari-seki* seats (cushions) surround the ring on four sides, with the *masu-seki* seats right behind them. The *masu-seki* seats are divided into "boxes" of four cushions, 130 cm by 125 cm. At the very back are boxes designed to seat 34 spectators, for a total seating capacity of 6,564.

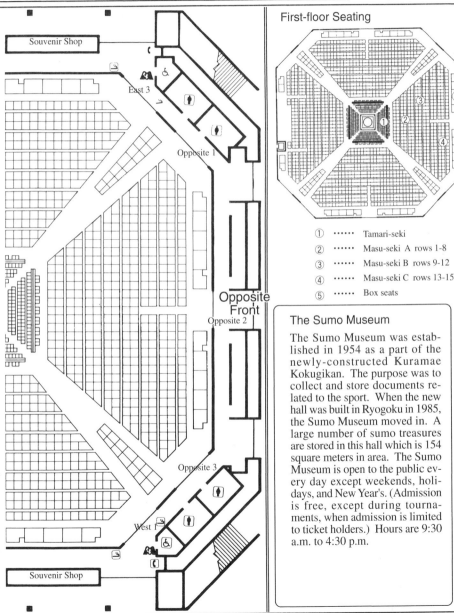

First-floor Seating

① ⋯⋯ Tamari-seki
② ⋯⋯ Masu-seki A rows 1-8
③ ⋯⋯ Masu-seki B rows 9-12
④ ⋯⋯ Masu-seki C rows 13-15
⑤ ⋯⋯ Box seats

The Sumo Museum

The Sumo Museum was established in 1954 as a part of the newly-constructed Kuramae Kokugikan. The purpose was to collect and store documents related to the sport. When the new hall was built in Ryogoku in 1985, the Sumo Museum moved in. A large number of sumo treasures are stored in this hall which is 154 square meters in area. The Sumo Museum is open to the public every day except weekends, holidays, and New Year's. (Admission is free, except during tournaments, when admission is limited to ticket holders.) Hours are 9:30 a.m. to 4:30 p.m.

to win one of three prizes given out daily. Look for the Morinaga Ballot Boxes located around the tournament hall, and make sure to get yours in by 3:00 p.m.

Second Floor Seating at the Ryogoku Kokugikan Hall

Morozashi

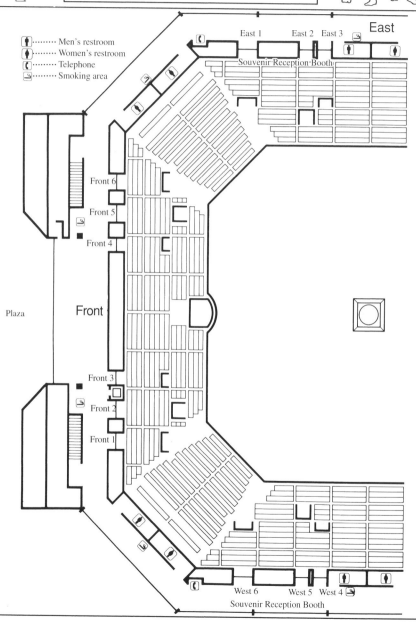

- 🚹 ········ Men's restroom
- 🚺 ········ Women's restroom
- 📞 ········ Telephone
- 🚬 ········ Smoking area

East 1   East 2   East 3   **East**

Souvenir Reception Booth

Front 6

Front 5

Front 4

Plaza

Front

Front 3

Front 2

Front 1

West 6   West 5   West 4

Souvenir Reception Booth

| Haridashi Information | When a new stable is built, there is a "ring-opening" ceremony held to celebrate the occasion. All of the gyoji from the clan bless the ring and a yokozuna performs his ring-entering ceremony. |

There are "chair" seats on all four sides of the Kokugikan Hall, with the Imperial Box in the middle of the "front" side. The rows are numbered from one to fourteen for a total of 4,534 seats. All the chairs have a width of 56 cm.

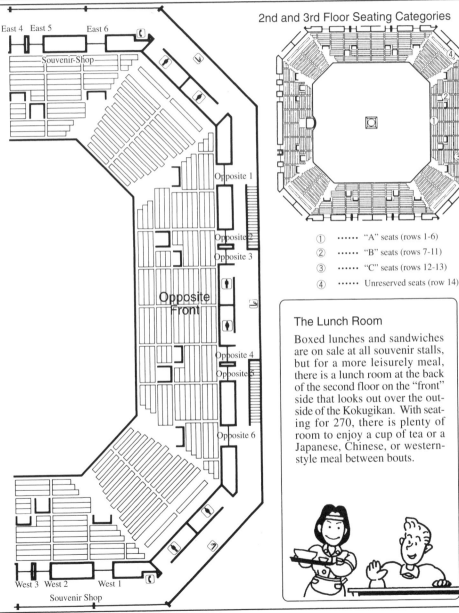

2nd and 3rd Floor Seating Categories

① ······ "A" seats (rows 1-6)
② ······ "B" seats (rows 7-11)
③ ······ "C" seats (rows 12-13)
④ ······ Unreserved seats (row 14)

The Lunch Room

Boxed lunches and sandwiches are on sale at all souvenir stalls, but for a more leisurely meal, there is a lunch room at the back of the second floor on the "front" side that looks out over the outside of the Kokugikan. With seating for 270, there is plenty of room to enjoy a cup of tea or a Japanese, Chinese, or western-style meal between bouts.

The Osaka Municipal Gymnasium

The Osaka Municipal Gymnasium

Address: 3-4-36 Namba-naka, Naniwa-ku, Osaka-shi 556-0011
Telephone no.: 06-631-0210

In 1987, remodeling of the Osaka Municipal Gym was completed at a cost of 12 billion yen. There are four floors above ground and two below with a total area of 29,000 square meters. For the Spring Tournament, the ring, dressing rooms, and other sumo-related facilities are installed on the second floor, with seating on the second, third, and fourth floors. The hall has an 8,500-person seating capacity, including standing room.

Ticket Prices

masu-seki A:	11,300 yen
masu-seki B:	10,300 yen
masu-seki C:	9,200 yen
Chair seats A	6,700 yen
Chair seats B	5,400 yen
Chair seats C	4,100 yen
Standing room:	adults 500 yen, children 200 yen

Neighborhood Map

The gym is a three-minute walk from the Midosuji, Yotsubashi, and Sennichimae subway stations, and the Namba, Nankai Honsen Namba, and Kintetsu Nara Line Namba train stations

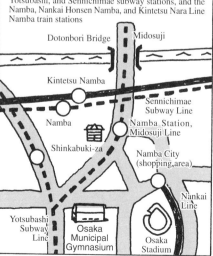

The March Tournament

三月場所

The Spring Tournament in Osaka

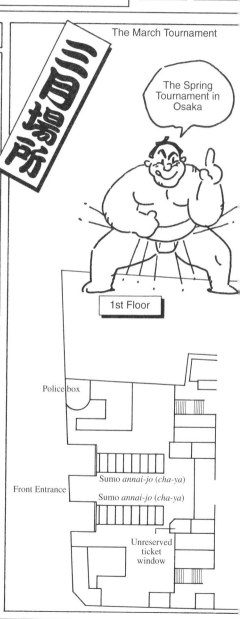

1st Floor

| **Haridashi Information** | Tickets for the March tournament (with the exception of unreserved) can now be purchased by telephone only. Lines are open from 9 a.m. to 5 p.m. every day until tickets are sold out. Telephone no: 06-636-4444.

The Spring Tournament, in March, has been held in Osaka at the Osaka Municipal Gymnasium ever since 1953 when the number of tournaments was increased to four a year. The gym was remodeled in 1985, with the Spring Tournament first held in the new structure in March 1987.

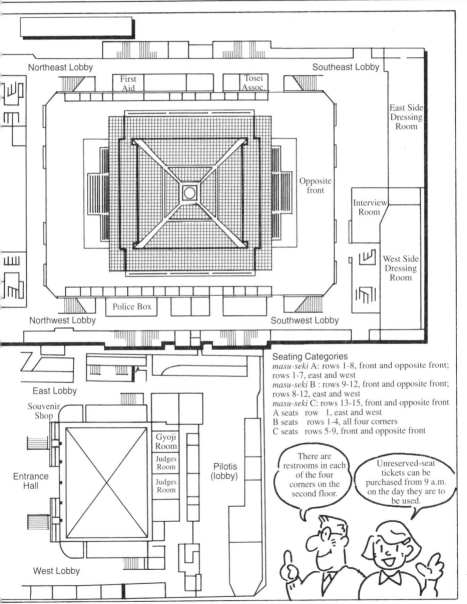

Northeast Lobby

First Aid

Tosei Assoc.

Southeast Lobby

East Side Dressing Room

Opposite front

Interview Room

West Side Dressing Room

Police Box

Northwest Lobby

Southwest Lobby

East Lobby

Souvenir Shop

Gyoji Room

Judges Room

Judges Room

Pilotis (lobby)

Entrance Hall

West Lobby

Seating Categories

masu-seki A: rows 1-8, front and opposite front; rows 1-7, east and west

masu-seki B : rows 9-12, front and opposite front; rows 8-12, east and west

masu-seki C: rows 13-15, front and opposite front

A seats   row 1, east and west

B seats   rows 1-4, all four corners

C seats   rows 5-9, front and opposite front

There are restrooms in each of the four corners on the second floor.

Unreserved-seat tickets can be purchased from 9 a.m. on the day they are to be used.

The Aiichi Prefectural Gymnasium

Winner's Flag

The Aiichi Prefectural Gymnasium

Address: 1-1 Ninomaru, Naka-ku, Nagoya-shi 460-0000
Telephone no.: 052-971-0015

The Aiichi Prefectural Gymnasium in Nagoya, completed in 1964, was built on the grounds of the Nagoya Castle Park. The large, open structure has three floors above ground and one below. Three powerful air conditioners maintain a temperature of 25 C. The ring, dressing rooms and other facilities are located on the first floor, with seating for 9000 fans on the first through third floors.

Ticket prices

masu-seki A: 11,300 yen
masu-seki B: 10,300 yen
masu-seki C: 9,200 yen
masu-seki D: 7,200 yen
Chair seats A: 4,700 yen
Chair seats B: adults 3,200 yen, children 200 yen

Neighborhood Map

The gym is a ten-minute taxi ride from the JR Nagoya Station, or a two-minute walk from the no. 7 exit of the Shiyakusho Station on the Meijo Subway Line, or a four-minute walk from the Higashi-otemae station on the Meitetsu Seto Train Line.

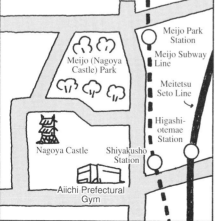

Meijo Park Station

Meijo Subway Line

Meitetsu Seto Line

Higashi-otemae Station

Meijo (Nagoya Castle) Park

Nagoya Castle

Shiyakusho Station

Aiichi Prefectural Gym

The July Tournament

七月場所

Entrance to 2nd floor

Sumo *annai-jo* (*cha-ya*)

Entrance to *masu-seki* (cushion box seats)

Entr

All the championship trophies are displayed in the show window

Front Plaza

Show Window

Group Ticket Window

Oh-h-h-Nagoya Castle..!

The Nagoya Tournament

Haridashi Information Tickets for all other tournaments go on sale a few weeks before a tournament begins. In the case of the Nagoya Tournament, however, sales begin in mid-March.

The July tournament (Nagoya Tournament) has been held since 1958. At first it was held in the Kanayama Gym. It was moved to its present location after the completion of the Nagoya Prefectural Gymnasium in 1965.

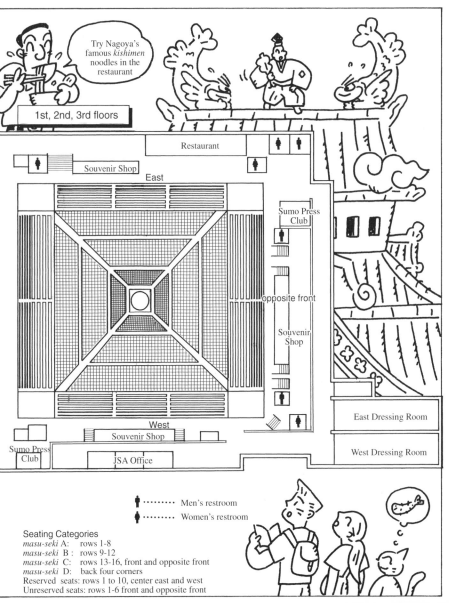

Try Nagoya's famous *kishimen* noodles in the restaurant

1st, 2nd, 3rd floors

Restaurant

Souvenir Shop

East

Sumo Press Club

opposite front

Souvenir Shop

West

Souvenir Shop

Sumo Press Club

JSA Office

East Dressing Room

West Dressing Room

♂ ········· Men's restroom
♀ ········· Women's restroom

Seating Categories
masu-seki A: rows 1-8
masu-seki B : rows 9-12
masu-seki C: rows 13-16, front and opposite front
masu-seki D: back four corners
Reserved seats: rows 1 to 10, center east and west
Unreserved seats: rows 1-6 front and opposite front

The Fukuoka Kokusai Center

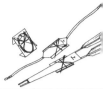

The Fukuoka Kokusai Center

Address: 2-2 Chikko-honmachi, Hakata-ku, Fukuoka-shi 812-0021
Telephone no.: 092-291-9311

The Fukuoka Kokusai Center was completed in 1981 at a cost of 3.8 billion yen. The steel and concrete structure has three floors above ground and one below. The hall air conditioning equipment is located in the basement. The ring, dressing rooms, and other offices, etc. are located on the first floor during the tournament, and the hall has a seating capacity of 9314, and 9774 when standing room is included.

Ticket Prices

masu-seki A: 11,300 yen
masu-seki B: 10,300 yen
masu-seki C: 9,200 yen
masu-seki D: 7,000 yen
A seats: 4,700 yen
B seats: adults 3,100 yen, children 200 yen

Neighborhood Map

A ten-minute taxi or bus ride from the JR Hakata Station (a two-minute walk from the Chikko-honmachi or Sekijo-machi bus stops). Or a ten-minute walk from the Nakasu-kawabata Station or Gofuku-machi Station on the No. 1 Subway Line.

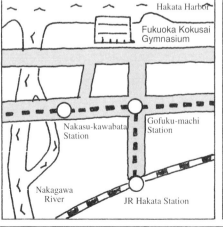

Hakata Harbor
Fukuoka Kokusai Gymnasium
Nakasu-kawabata Station
Gofuku-machi Station
Nakagawa River
JR Hakata Station

十一月場所

November Tournament

Center offices

Vending machines

Entrance Hall

In the entrance hall, portraits of the winners of the Kyushu Tournament are on display.

JSA Office

Vending machines

Souvenir shop

Police

Special buses pick up passengers as soon as the day's bouts are over.

Taxi stand
Bus stop

Haridashi Information | There is a festival the night before the opening of the Kyushu Tournament. There are drum performances, rikishi singing contests, the introduction of rikishi from the Kyushu area, and other attractions.

The November tournament (Kyushu Tournament) was first held as a regularly-scheduled event in 1957 at the Fukuoka Sports Center. It was moved to the Kyuden Memorial Gymnasium in 1974. The tournament arrived at its present location, the Fukuoka Kokusai Center, in 1981.

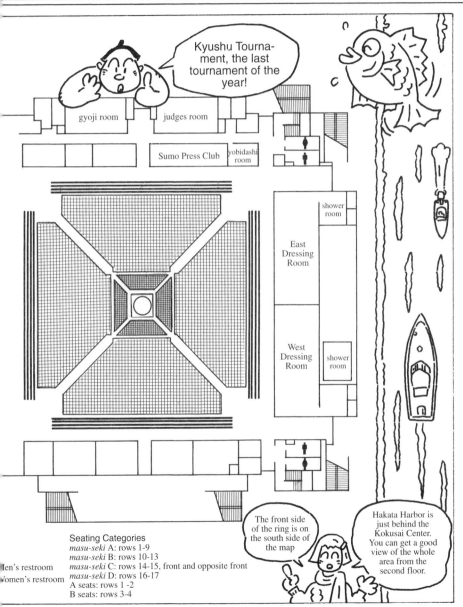

Kyushu Tournament, the last tournament of the year!

gyoji room

judges room

Sumo Press Club

yobidashi room

shower room

East Dressing Room

West Dressing Room

shower room

The front side of the ring is on the south side of the map

Hakata Harbor is just behind the Kokusai Center. You can get a good view of the whole area from the second floor.

Seating Categories
masu-seki A: rows 1-9
masu-seki B: rows 10-13
masu-seki C: rows 14-15, front and opposite front
masu-seki D: rows 16-17
A seats: rows 1 -2
B seats: rows 3-4

Men's restroom
Women's restroom

Sumo Dictionary

A glossary of phrases used in the sumo world

Ago o kamasu (uppercut)
To refuse a request in a cold manner. Another way of expressing the same this is *teppo kamaseru* (shooting a rifle).

Aikuchi
The "karma" between oneself and another wrestler that has nothing to do with rank or ability. When a wrestler has an opponent that he can never manage to beat, he says it is *aikuchi ga warui*, or a bad match. Of a wrestler he finds easy to beat, he will say *aikuchi ga warui*, or a good match.

Amma or Momu (both mean "massage")
Term for an upper-level rikishi giving a lower-level rikishi a training session.

Appa
A rikishi wife. Wives of stablemasters are referred to with greater respect as *o-kami-san*.

Banzai
Losing one's grip on an opponent so that one's arms are left in the air.

Bariki (horse power)
Liquor. Drinking liquor is referred to as "adding horse power."

Bimbo-gami (god of the paupers)
The top juryo-rank rikishi. This unflattering nickname derives from the fact that the rikishi in this position is frequently called upon to wrestle top-ranked rikishi but never for more than the juryo salary.

Bonnaka (in a tray)
To be considerate.

Burutakaru (want to quake)
Being afraid of one's opponent. A feeling of fear.

Chikara-ashi (strong foot)
To stamp

Chikara-zumo (strong sumo)
Wrestling with strength rather than technique

Dashippei (protruding paper)
The ritual papers on two rods attached to the scaffolding for the drums.

Deashi (forward foot)
Moving a foot forward in a manner that is very basic and practical for wrestling.

Densha-michi (train tracks)
To run an opponent straight out of the ring as soon as a bout begins.

Dokkoi (do it)
A stubborn person. Someone who gets his own way knowing full well that he is mistaken. Forcing a mistaken action through to completion is called " doing a *dokkoi* ."

Ebisuko (god of wealth)
Eating till one is full. If someone regularly eats a lot, it is said that he is "good at *ebisuko*."

Fumi kiri (railroad crossing)
When the front half of the foot lands just outside the ring.

Fumi koshi (over the tracks)
When the whole foot is out of the ring.

Gachinko (crash bang)
Meeting an opponent (or any other challenge) head on.

Gainisuru (cause damage)
Go after with a vengeance. Fierce practice sessions.

Sumo Dictionary

Ginnagashi (flowing silver)
To dress up or otherwise act as though one has a lot of money.

Goningakari (taking on five)
Often seen in exhibition matches. A yokozuna or other upper-ranked rikishi will take on five trainees, fighting them all off at once.

Gonosen (last is first)
A rikishi who manages to maneuver himself into an advantageous position even though he was slow at the outset of a bout.

Gottsan
The most often-used word for "thank you."

Gyaku-ashi (backward feet)
The opposite of a basic position. Putting the left foot forward when grabbing an opponent's belt with the right hand, and so on.

Gyoji-kuroboshi (Gyoji Black Star)
Reversal of a gyoji decission.

Hagami
A signed verification of a loan. Borrowing money is referred to as "entering a *hagami*."

Hakite (brush hand)
Describes the hand of a rikishi when it brushes the floor of the ring lightly during a bout.

Hakoyama (box mountain)
Used to refer to the sumo hair dresser, also called *yama* for short.

Hanpa-zumo (watered-down sumo)
A rikishi who does not have a good grasp of sumo basics.

Sumo Dictionary

Hazu-ni-kakaru
Happening to get in on a free meal. Eating for free.

Henoko-zashi (a bent rod)
A wooden pointer. (Henoko refers to a penis. The same as kataguchi).

Hitachigata
A braggart, someone who tries to show himself up as better than he is.

Hinoshita Kaisan (the open mountain under the sun)
A nickname for an unusually strong person. Usually refers to a yokozuna.

Hippari-komu
Pull one's opponent in and grab his belt.

Hitachigata
A braggart, someone who tries to show himself up as better than he is.

Hoshi (star)
A woman or a girlfriend.

Iitoko uru (selling the good parts)
Bragging and pretending to know more than one really does; relating events in an amusing manner.

Ikitai or Kitai (living body)
A rikishi in a position in which a win is even remotely possible. The opposite of this, naturally, is "shinitai" or "shitai" (corpse)

Iregake
Cancellation of a match during a tour because of rain, etc. If there is room in the schedule, these outdoor events can be held the next day. Otherwise, money has to be returned.

Jun-honbasho (practice tournament)
A touring competition that is like a regular tournament, but has no effect on a rikishi's win-loss record.

Kamo no irekubi (collaring the duck)
A position in which both wrestlers have their upper bodies bent and their heads on each others' shoulders; they each have a grasp of their opponent's thrusting arm and are both pushing. Also called *shishi no taninozoki* (lions peeking into the valley).

Kao ja nai (not his face)
Someone who does not look capable of handling what he is up against.

Karada-make (lose to a body)
To lose a bout because of a difference in size.

Kataguchi (shoulder)
Penis

Katasukashi o kurau (dodging)
To evade requests using tricks or lies

Katayairi (entrance of the big man)
Another name for the entrance of a yokozuna

Kawaigaru (to dote)
A higher-ranked rikishi giving a lower one a painful training session.

Keikozumo (training sumo)
Exhibition training sessions called *hanazumo*.

Kengamine (sink or swim)
Being perched on the bales that make up the ring; a critical position.

Keshodachi (cosmetic appearance)
Displaying a tough attitude even if there is no will to back it up.

Ki-ga-jukusu (feeling gets ripe)
The condition of two rikishi just before facing off.

Kiai (spirit)
The spiritual and mental power to meet challenges head on. Rikishi say they are "adding spirit" or they "can feel the spirit come."

Kidogomen (free admission)
Special permission for persons who have supported the Japan Sumo Association for many years to attend tournaments for free. These supporters receive a special badge in honor of the privilege.

Kimake (lack of spirit)
Losing a bout because of a lack of spirit and determination.

Kimeru (to decide)
Used instead of the verb "to do."

Kinboshi (Gold Star)
A beautiful woman.

Kitamuki (facing north)
A quarrelsome person.

Koen-kai (support group)
An organization joined in its spiritual and material support of either a single rikishi or an entire stable. Each group has its own operational methods, etc.

Komebitsu (rice dispenser)
The sekitori who is the cornerstone of a stable; the one who brings in the money.

Konpachi (snap)
When a rikishi has grown his hair long enough to tie it into a chonmage topknot, he goes and shows it to his immediate "superior." This "big brother apprentice" then snaps his fingers against the other's forehead before giving him a small present to celebrate the event.

Koshi o waru (break one's back)
Spread one's legs out as far as possible, bend the knees, and try to bring one's weight down as low as possible.

Kubinage (neck throw)
To have a relationship with a women.

Kuisagaru (refuse to let go)
A wrestling position in which a rikishi lowers his head beneath the level of his opponent's chest, lowering his back as he does so.

Me ga hiraku (opening the eyes)
Getting one's first win of a tournament. This is also called *shonichi o dasu*, or "putting out the first day."

Miyazumo (court sumo)
Benefit sumo performed at a shrine.

Mochidai (money for rice cakes)
Bonuses given to elders by the JSA.

Mukouzuke (turned backwards)
Grabbing the front of an opponent's belt with both hands and leaning one's head into his chest.

Mune wo awaseru (matching of chests)
A position in which two opponents have a grip on each other's belts and their bodies are pressed up against each other.

Mune wo dasu (sticking out one's chest)
Allowing fellow rikishi   the use of one's chest during impact practice. Also called *mune o kasu* or "lending one's chest."

Naiki (inside rules)
Unwritten rules of the JSA.

Namakura-yotsu
Not favoring a grip with one hand over the other.

Nanori (calling out one's own name; especially in battle)
Another word for *shikona* or "wrestling name."

Nicho (two servings)
Both feet.

Nimai-kansatsu (two tags)
An obsolete practice in which an active rikishi could own elder stock and be listed on the ranking chart as both a rikishi and an elder.

Nuke-nuke (skip-skip)
When east and west take every other bout from each other; or winning every other day.

Ogappei (big merger)
A touring group consisting of all the sumo stables. A "big merger tour."

Ogashira (big chief)
The top-ranking rikishi at the makushita rank.

Okome (rice)
Money. Usually refers to a salary or allowance.

On wo kaesu (returning a favor)
Beating a rikishi of higher rank during a practice bout, or passing him up on the ranking chart.

Otenki (good weather)
Having no money. Also called *oteagari* (hands up).

Ottsukeru (force on)
Being treated to something. Also called *osu*, or "push."

Ryobari (boxing both)
Boxing both of an opponent's ears simultaneously. This is another prohibited move.

Sagari wo sabaku (rowing the strands)
Dividing the strands on a mawashi to the right and left when beginning a bout.

Sakadori (backwards schedule)
During tours where exhibitions are held outdoors, the schedule may be reversed and the yokozuna and san'yaku bouts held first if it looks as if the weather is not going to hold out.

Sakawari (backwards split)
Returning part of one's salary to the union if an exhibition tour ends in the red.

Sekitan taku (burning coal)
Doing something in a big rush.

Shide
The folded paper chains hung from the ceremonial rope of the yokozuna. There are five strands, each with four rectangles of paper attached.

Shika wo kimeru (make like a deer)
To pretend not to know something or someone.

Shikakusha (person with a license)
Usually means an elder who is eligible to receive a pension. It is can also refer to a makuuchi wrestler.

Shogoban (proper no. 5)
A form of competition often used in touring exhibitions. Ten rikishi are divided into two teams. The first two face off, with the winner fighting the next person on the opposing team. The bouts continue until all of the members of one team have lost and been eliminated.

Sumo Dictionary

Tachiai-make (losing the tachiai)
Being attacked by an opponent at the onset of the bout and losing the adventage to him.

Taguru (reel in)
Putting an opponent off guard by pulling his attacking arm towards oneself.

Tai wo azukeru (entrust one's body)
Shoving an opponent with one's whole body.

Tako ni naru (make like an octopus)
To be snooty.

Tamari-seki
The spectator seats immediately surrounding the ring; also known as *suna-kaburi* or "drenched with sand."

Tanimachi(sponsor)
A sumo supporter, one who gives financial support to an individual wrestler or stable.

Teyotsu (four hands)
An offensive position in which both rikishi hold onto each other's hands. Also called *teguruma* or "hand wheel."

Tezumo (hand sumo)
A term used to refer to a touring event run by the JSA rather than by a local sponsor. Eating or drinking at one's own expense.

Tobitsuki (running jump)
Pre-sumo and some practice sessions that are begun without the preliminary face off.

Tonpachi
Someone who cannot see two feet in front of himself; a person with poor intuition.

Shiranui-Type

Tsurazumo (face sumo)
To win and then keep on winning, or to lose and continue to lose.

Ukisoku (floating leg)
Picking one's leg up from the ring in a disadvantageous manner.

Waki ga amai (weak on the side)
Being attacked by an opponent because one failed to keep his arms down tight enough.

Yachin ga takai (rent is expensive)
A situation in which the rank of a rikishi is higher than he can maintain on his own power and he consequently begins to lose most of his bouts.

Yakata (house)
Refers to the roof over the ring. The roof used to be supported by four columns which were removed in 1952 when the roof was hung from the roof of the building.

Yamaiku (get sick)
Injuries.

Yubitori (finger taker)
Bending back the finger of an opponent. This is a prohibited move.

Yumifuri (bow swinger)
Performing the bow-twirling ceremony at the end of each tournament day. The rikishi who performs this ceremony.

Zutsuki o kamasu
Being soundly scolded. Being scolded is *zutsuki o kurau*.